GROW YOUR OWN
PHARMACY

51 HEALING PLANTS AND
HOW TO USE THEM

SUSAN PATTERSON

MASTER GARDENER

BACKYARD
·VITALITY·

CONTENTS

Foreword

Some of my very best friends are plants. Don't get me wrong, I've got some very good human (and a few canine) friends, too … but my relationships with my botanical buddies are special and unique.

Some of them live nearby, like the lovely Echinacea, Lavender, or Elderberry in my backyard … or the stubborn Dandelion in the front. Some of them are wild, like the St. John's Wort that blooms next to the sidewalk every year in June, or the Blackberries and Sumac we find on our daily hikes near the lake. Some of them are old friends like Calendula or Comfrey in the herb garden and some of them are more recent acquaintances like the Aronia berries growing against the back fence. Some of them live right inside with my family … on windowsills or under lights like the Patchouli and Jasmine in my bedroom.

Just like my human friends, some of my plant friends are polite and well behaved like Rosemary. Others are wild and unruly like Nettles. Some are gentle and kind like Lemon Balm. Others are toxic and can even be dangerous like Foxglove. Some stay close to home and others live really far away. Some like it cold. And yes, just like humans, some like it hot.

I know most of my plant friends by their fancy Latin names, but I call most of them by their more familiar nicknames. Each one has a distinct personality - and of course a unique look, smell, taste, and purpose.

These botanical friends are actually more than friends, they're my allies. They have fed me, they have helped me and my family recover from illness, they have been my most important tools as a naturopathic physician, and they've been there for comfort in times of sorrow and to offer joy in times of celebration.

Knowing, growing, and using medicinal herbs has been a lifelong journey for me and I can assure you that if I had a book like the one you have in your hands right now ... I would be much further along than I am today! This book is a masterclass (by a real master gardener) that will help you become fast friends with so many of the plants that I have come to know and love. For each one, you'll get a sense of its history and medicinal properties, and how to start, grow, harvest, store and use the herb in your own life. I trust that each one will become a new friend of yours ... as they have for me.

I'm grateful that my human friend Susan has written this book to help introduce you to a few of our favorite plant friends - the more friends the better! I think we'll all get along great.

-Joshua Levitt, ND

Preface

Plants are highly complex and truly remarkable. They are the only living things that can make their own energy using the light from the sun. All other living things, human and animal, require plants to provide us the energy and nutrients we need for survival.

....

Much of my medicinal plant knowledge came from a group of older women who were pillars of the *West Virginia Herb Association*. Each month, we would meet to share our love of plants. I would listen intently as they talked about foraging, growing, and identifying plants and crafting their favorite home remedies, including elixirs, creams, salves, tinctures, honey, butter, jams, jellies, and even liquors. Their passion for and knowledge of plants was rooted deep in their heritage, passed down through generations. It was here, surrounded by such rich culture, timeless tales, and respect, that I genuinely understood and fell in love with the power of medicinal plants. For four years, I tagged along with my notebook in tow, writing, drawing, and absorbing everything I could. When I tried to thank them for all they had taught me, they only smiled and said, *"You never thank anyone for giving you a plant or plant knowledge; you just keep passing it on."*

Fast forward twenty years. Many of my former herb association friends are now gone, but their stories live on. I am still amazed by herbs - their beauty, their strength, and their immense value. I often find myself plucking a peppermint leaf, rolling it between my fingers, taking in the exciting aroma, and thinking of the many valuable compounds it contains. A cup of freshly brewed chamomile tea instantly transports me to the garden - even in the dead of winter. In my mind, I can still see the cellars belonging to my herb-loving friends, stacked to the brim with drying plants and many jars of neatly labeled leaves, buds, roots, and stems. What a beautiful sight to behold!

This book is just one of the ways that I am *"passing it on."* It is for anyone who wants to do a deep dive into the vast world of healing plants. Remember, you don't have to be a seasoned gardener to read and enjoy this book. I hope that after you have finished taking it all in - you will be, like me, amazed at the power of plants!

In this book, I focus on plants that I have grown and used before and those that I know are fantastic additions to any home pharmacy garden. Use this information as a springboard to dive deeper, learn more, and broaden your understanding and appreciation for plants so you too can *"pass it on!"*

Most of all, have fun and happy growing!

Susan Patterson Stevens, CBHC and Master Gardener

A Cautionary Note

Although most herbs are safe, you have to be highly cautious, as some herbal preparations can be toxic and cause allergic reactions or interfere with the medicine you are taking. Here are some things to keep in mind when considering using herbal preparations.

- **Educate** yourself and learn as much as you can about herbs and their medicinal properties and uses.

- Work with a **trained and licensed herbalist** or naturopathic doctor who has extensive training and experience in the use of herbal remedies.

- Use herbs for **minor ailments only** – not severe or life-threatening conditions.

- Use only the **recommended amounts** for the suggested time.

- Use the **correct herbs** – seek guidance if necessary from a professional herbalist.

- Always use the **correct part** of the plant.

- Always start with a **small amount** of herb if it is your first time using it.

- **Don't** use herbs if you are pregnant or nursing.

- **Consult** a healthcare practitioner before giving herbs to children.

- **Don't forage** for medicinal plants in unknown locations.

Plant Power

A brief historical overview of medicinal plants

....

"Herbs are the friend of the physician and the pride of cooks."

- Charlemagne

Plants are powerful, more so than you could ever imagine. They have the power to cure, and they have the power to kill. Herbs are widely recognized as plants with a purpose (although I might argue that all plants have a purpose), whose leaves, seeds, and flowers are used for flavoring, food, medicine, or perfume.

Throughout history, doctors, philosophers, and great thinkers have recognized the importance of herbs in medicine. Hippocrates, the *"Father of Medicine,"* classified 300-400 species of herbs into their essential qualities and created a diagnosis and prognosis system using herbs.

The great philosopher Aristotle compiled a list of medicinal plants. His best student, Theophrastus, researched herbs as medicine, carefully studying parts of plants used, collection methods, and their impact on humans and animals. He is credited with founding the science of botany which included in-depth descriptions of medicinal plants growing in botanical gardens in Athens.

The Roman army physician, Dioscorides, wrote ***De Materia Medica*** around AD 60. In this massive, five-volume compilation, he discussed 500 plants and described how to make 1,000 simple drugs. This incredible, extensive work was written in Greek and contained descriptions of plants, including their origins and medicinal properties, and was used as a standard text for 1,500 years!

Historical records of Native American, Roman, Egyptian, Persian, and Hebrew medicine show that herbs were an integral part of ancient medical practices and were used to treat almost every known illness.

According to Ayurvedic theory, illness is an imbalance in the body, and herbs and dietary controls can help restore this essential balance. Abdullah Ben Ahmad Al Bitar was an Arabic botanist and pharmaceutical scientist in the 13th century who wrote the ***Explanation of Dioscorides Book on Herbs***. He also compiled ***The Glossary of Drugs and Food Vocabulary*** that contains the names and uses of 1,400 drugs, foods, and plants.

In 1775, as modern medical techniques began to advance, Dr. William Withering, an English geologist, botanist, chemist, and physician, was treating a patient with edema (dropsy) from heart failure. During his treatment, the administration of traditional medicine by the doctor brought about no change. However, an herbal brew based on an old family recipe was given to the patient by his family, and he began to recover.

After this, Dr. Withering began experimenting with the herbs contained in the recipe and found that foxglove was a significant medicinal powerhouse. After this discovery, he spent the next ten years studying foxglove, and his *Account of the Foxglove and Some of its Medical Uses* was published in 1785. In this book, he outlined 200 cases where foxglove was used to treat edema and heart failure successfully. Eventually, the cardiac glycosides, digoxin, and digitoxin were identified as the key compounds in and were extracted from the plant. These are still used in treating heart conditions today.

Synthetic versions do not always have the same medicinal punch and can even present adverse side effects when used apart from the entire plant.

Herbal remedies were widely used in America until the early 1900s, when the modern pharmaceutical industry began to isolate individual active compounds and create drugs around them. The first drug isolated from a plant was morphine in 1803 by Frederich Serturner in Germany. Soon other scientists followed, using similar techniques to extract drugs from plants. In 1852, salicin, the active ingredient in willow bark, was extracted. By 1880, Bayer modified the extract into a milder form, and aspirin was conceived.

This was the beginning of a medical system known as allopathy. Allopathy refers to Western medicine or to any treatment that is not homeopathic or natural. The excessive use of manufactured medication in our world today and the departure from plants as medicine have created a society reliant on synthetic, commercial drugs. While many of these drugs are critical and lifesaving, the immense value and contribution of herbs must not be overlooked.

Herbs contain synergists, buffers, and counterbalances that work together with the more powerful ingredients. When herbs are used in their complete form, the body's natural healing process utilizes all parts to balance the body and restore health.

Because herbal remedies and supplements are not under the "watchful" eyes of the FDA or other governing agencies, their use remains controversial among certain groups - despite the long history of successful study and use by generations of doctors and great thinkers.

Naturopaths, functional medical practitioners, and herbalists commonly use plant medicine for primary and supplementary therapy. Herbal remedies can help nourish the immune system, stimulate new liver tissue, increase the strength of the adrenal glands, and counterbalance the adverse effects of chemical treatments. They can also balance the endocrine system, fend off bacteria, relieve anxiety, improve sleep, speed up fat burning, balance blood sugar, and improve brain function, among other things. The power of plants is nothing short of amazing, a fact clearly evidenced in our predecessors' research and modern scientific study.

The great news is, medicinal plant power is not just reserved for professionals. It is completely accessible to home gardeners and those interested in natural remedies. In fact, when you consider adding medicinal plants to your home garden, a whole new world of possibilities opens up in your very own backyard pharmacy!

"My opinion, however, is that they (herbs) are superior 95% of the time to any pharmaceutical drug!"
- Robert Willner MD

Growing Medicinal Plants in the Home Garden

Although you can forage for many medicinal plants, growing them in your home garden allows easy access for remedies. Plus, you get the added pleasure of planting and caring for your botanical beauties.

Planting location, amount of sun, watering, and harvesting time, among other factors, are all essential to take into consideration when growing herbs. Here are a few tips for success that I have learned from trial and error throughout the years.

Seed Starting

Starting seeds is an exciting time. It is filled with anticipation for the start of the official gardening season and excitement over watching your seeds grow into hearty seedlings that will populate your garden. Here are a few tricks that may come in handy this seed-starting season:

- Be sure to use a high-quality seed-starter mix to give your young plants the best chance to survive.

- Choose a nice, sunny day to start your seeds so that you can prepare your soil and fill your containers outdoors.

- You don't need expensive grow lights or heating mats. Simple, low-hanging shop lights will work just as well. You should keep about an inch of space between the highest leaves and the light. Raise the light as the seedlings grow to maintain this distance.

- Use labels to identify what seeds you are growing, or simply write it on the container with a permanent marker.

- Moisten the soil before planting. It should be wet but not dripping. You should also lightly mist your seeds after planting.

- Use a lid or plastic wrap over your containers until the seeds sprout. This will help encourage germination and trap moisture.

- Though it may seem counterintuitive to remove a plant, thinning your seedlings is essential for the health of your crop. If two seeds are growing in a single container, simply snip off the weaker or smaller one at the soil level.

If you are looking for ways to be frugal, recycle household goods, and start seeds without breaking the bank, these budget-friendly, creative ideas will set you on your way.

K-cups

While there is some concern about K-cups' environmental and health impact, there's no denying that they are convenient. If you still use these handy single-serve coffee containers, try repurposing them into seed starting containers. Simply line them up on an old cookie tray to make them easy to move, fill the cups with soil, and pop in your seeds. Remember, these cups are not biodegradable, so unlike other seed-starting containers, the plant will need to be removed from the cup before being planted outside.

Egg cartons

Though an egg carton is slightly small to use as a starting container for many veggies, it makes the perfect choice for herbs such as basil and cilantro. Plus, it is thin and can fit in a windowsill, which is a bonus if you don't have a lot of extra table space near a window and don't want to set up a grow light. If you do stick it in a windowsill, make sure that it isn't drafty, as the cold, early spring air could kill your seedlings.

Simply cut the carton in half, fill the bottom of one side with your soil and seeds, line the other half with a thin layer of plastic, and then situate the sides inside of each other. You should now have an egg carton half with soil and seeds and the remaining egg carton half lined with plastic underneath. This will help prevent leakage as the material breaks down.

Paper towel and toilet paper rolls

Cut down cardboard rolls to your desired size and line them up on a plastic tray. Since these containers won't have a bottom, it is important to avoid lifting them up and moving them as much as you can. One of the greatest things about using cardboard to start seedlings is that you can plant the whole thing when moving your seedlings outdoors; no transplanting needed. It's super easy to save cardboard tubes, and you won't have to spend a penny!

Plants with smaller roots, such as tomatoes, work best in toilet paper tubes as they won't break out of the bottom. I also love cardboard tubes because you can simply add some water to the tray and hydrate your seedlings from the bottom up without having to worry about disturbing their delicate growth.

Plastic nursery pots

Plastic pots are incredibly useful, so if you're throwing away your containers after planting, you are making a huge mistake. When you buy plants from a nursery, they will usually come in plastic cups joined together or flimsy, individual pots. These make the perfect seed-starting containers!

Yogurt containers

Single-serve yogurt cups, sour cream containers, and other recycled plastic containers are excellent for seed starting. Rinse them out thoroughly, let them dry, and fill them with soil and plant your seeds. Bigger containers don't need to be filled all the way, but it is a good idea to cut them down to just above the soil line so that the light can still reach the seeds. Another benefit of soft plastic containers is that you can easily squeeze them and dislodge the soil without disturbing the roots, which makes transplanting a breeze.

....

You can have the best seed starting method available and follow all of the steps above to a T; however, without hardening off your seedlings, you will likely be facing serious disappointment when they succumb to the elements after you try to plant them in the garden. Hardening off is the process where seedlings grown indoors are introduced to the outdoors in preparation for transplant. Without hardening off, young plants can quickly go into shock and even die. To guarantee the best results possible with young plants, it is always wise to go through a hardening off process.

Here's how to best harden off your little plants and ease their transition into the garden.

Hardening Off

Hardening off your seedlings is the best thing you can do to prepare them for the harsh, unforgiving outside world that is so different from their carefully regulated indoor environment. Instead of simply sticking them in the ground (which is just setting them up for failure), take the time to acclimate them to things like wind, rain, and inconsistent sunlight to help them grow stronger and withstand environmental extremes. Follow these simple steps to harden off medicinal plants and help them thrive.

- **Take your time:** Hardening off seedlings isn't something that should be rushed in a matter of days. Take your time and begin the process at least two weeks before you plan to plant your babies outdoors. Follow planting guidelines for each particular plant to determine the date you should begin hardening off. This time is usually known as the frost date and should be indicated on the seed packet.

- **Stop coddling:** Once plants are left outside, they will have to pretty much fend for themselves other than some occasional watering and feeding. This is unlike their early weeks, where you paid close attention to the burgeoning sprouts, and it can often be a shock to the seedlings. Begin the hardening off process by ceasing any supplemental watering or feeding about a week before they go outside.

- **Start slow:** Place your seedlings in an open box to make it easier to cart them back and forth. The box will also help act as a windbreak and prevent moisture evaporation, which can quickly kill delicate seedlings. Place the box in a slightly sheltered area to begin (usually a little shade is a good idea) and leave your seedlings there for a few hours. Increase the time each day for a week until your seedlings are outside for around eight to nine hours.

- **Bring it up a notch:** During the next week of the hardening off process, keep your box in the shade, move it to the sun for a few hours, and then back to the shade. Follow the same process, increasing by an hour every day until your plant is spending the whole day in the bright sun. Continue bringing the box in at night while you are hardening them off.

- **Plant them:** Once your little seedlings have gotten used to the sun, wind, rain, and chill of the great outdoors, it is time to plant them in the garden. Keep them moist and give them a dose of fertilizer to help set them up for success. If you are still experiencing chilly nights, it may be a good idea to cover them with fleece or row covers for a few weeks. Follow planting instructions, and don't be discouraged if every seedling doesn't survive. But, if you followed the hardening off instructions, your seedlings should be sturdy, and ready to grow into healthy, productive plants.

Note on greenhouses

Using a greenhouse or cold frame to harden off seedlings is an excellent idea if you have one available. Follow the same basic premise, but instead of moving your seedlings inside, simply prop open the cover on the cold frame or leave the door to the greenhouse open during the day. This is usually more convenient and will allow you to grow many seedlings without having to worry about indoor growing space and setting up a UV light system. If you are growing seedlings in a greenhouse, keep it heated in the early spring and begin to cut back on the heat as you harden off your baby plants.

Dividing Plants

Starting seeds can be thrilling - watching the seeds grow and sprout and mature into full-fledged herbs is a gratifying experience. But the real fun begins when your established plants are able to create more and more plants that you can give away or use in other areas in your garden. Whether you propagate through stem cuttings or stick with root division, herbs will be the gifts that keep on giving.

Stem Cuttings

One of the most cost-effective ways to start new herbs is to use stem cuttings. This technique is simple, and once mastered, works on any perennial plant that has a stalk. The best herbs (included in this book) to propagate using cuttings include:

- Basil
- Lavender
- Lemon Balm
- Lemon Verbena
- Mint
- Oregano
- Rosemary
- Sage
- Stevia
- Tarragon
- Thyme

When to take a cutting

The absolute best time to take a cutting from any plant is when it is actively growing but not flowering. If there are flowers on any stem piece, remove them. Take cuttings in the morning, as this is less stressful on the plant. Be sure to cut with clean, well-disinfected cutting tools and clean before and after cutting when changing between plants.

Where to take a cutting

Take a close look at your plant stem; there will be a "*softwood*" and a "*hardwood*" section - softwood is lighter in color and more flexible. This is the new growth, and new growth roots easier than old growth.

How to take a cutting

Cut under the place where the leaves join the stem - this is called a node. Take a four to six-inch cutting. Pinch the leaves off the bottom two inches of your cutting. New roots will emerge from this spot.

Root the cuttings

Some herb cuttings like sage, thyme, mint, basil, oregano, stevia, and lemon balm will quickly root when placed in a jar with water. Others do best when planted directly into the soil. For those you root in water, be sure to place the jar in indirect light and change the water daily. Once new roots have formed, plant the cutting in a container filled with potting soil. Keep the plant indoors for at least two to four weeks before transplanting.

For container planting, use a damp rooting medium composed of equal parts perlite and vermiculite. Place the cutting into the planting medium, leaving the top part with leaves exposed. Set the container in a warm location that receives indirect light. Cover the pot with a clear plastic bag or growing dome. Keep the planting medium moist but not soggy. Open the bag daily for a few minutes to promote air circulation. Once the cutting has formed roots tug lightly on the cutting to check for roots. Resistance is a positive sign, re-pot each cutting into a new pot filled with potting soil. Allow two to four weeks of growth before transplanting into the garden.

Note:

Softwood cuttings root well without rooting hormone - use this for hardwood cuttings only.

Root Division

Several perennial herbs can be easily divided by simply splitting their roots. Here are some great ones to try:

- Chamomile
- Chives
- Marjoram
- Mint
- Oregano
- Sage
- Tarragon
- Thyme

When to divide

Divide perennial herbs between early fall and mid-spring, depending on your growing season and weather conditions. Fall is a good time in milder locations, but early spring is best in those areas with cooler temperatures. Dividing at the wrong time can disrupt plant growth. To keep your herbs looking their best, divide them every two to four years.

How to divide

Use a clean shovel or sharp knife to divide. Remove mulch and other debris from around the base of the plant. Dig gently around the plant and lift the root ball from the soil. Grasp the clump and divide it using your shovel or knife. Depending on the size of the parent plant, make two or three divisions. Each divided section should have roots and shoots.

How to replant

Replant the sections as soon as you can - in fact, it is a good idea to choose your location and get your new hole ready before dividing. If you can't plant right away, place the roots in water to keep them from drying out. As soon as you have replanted your new division, water it well and apply a two inch layer of mulch.

The rest of this section will prepare you for optimal success in your herb garden.

Vigorous Plants

Some herbs are notorious for their prolific growth. They spread in all directions, sending out runners or sprouting roots from wherever their stems touch the soil. Common mint and many of its relatives are typical examples. Given half a chance, they will take over your entire garden and become a menace for years to come. At the same time, no herb garden is complete without them. Growing these herbs in pots, large tubs, or other similar containers is the best solution. You can recess the containers in the ground if you want; just be sure that you use separate containers for different kinds of mint.

Confining invasive herbs in containers does not work for plants that spread by self-seeding. For instance, chives, lemon balm, chamomile, and comfrey, spread their seeds far and wide, and you'll end up with seedlings popping up all over the place. Your only option is to prevent them from setting seeds by either harvesting them before they flower or removing flowers as soon as they open.

Sun Matters

Many herbs that have become an essential part of our cuisine originated in the sunny Mediterranean region. This area is characterized by warm winters, hot summers, and clear, bright skies. Thyme, parsley, basil, rosemary, sage, and oregano are typical examples. Although they have adapted well to different growing conditions in many foreign lands, they thrive when they're provided with their native environment. Plenty of sunlight is one of their basic requirements, and warmth is another. That's why they grow well during spring and summer but start to decline as fall progresses toward a cold winter.

Some herbs like mint, garlic, chives, oregano, and lemon balm do well in the sun and partial shade. In fact, the vigorous growth of many sun-loving herbs can be curbed by growing them in the shade. Many herbs belonging to the carrot family, such as parsley,  cilantro, and chervil, often suffer when they are planted in fully exposed areas, especially under the hot summer sun. Providing some afternoon shade is ideal for those types of herbs.

Water Rules

Unlike your vegetables and ornamental plants that may only need to be watered two or three times a week, herbs are happier with daily watering. For one, most of them have a root system that's confined to the top layers of soil. Since the topsoil dries out very fast, the plants become water-stressed and will begin to wilt. They may revive as soon as you give them water, but frequent wilting can make many herbs bitter. The stems also become woody as they develop more support tissue to withstand water stress.

Wilting cycles can cause premature aging in some herbs. They interpret these temporary drought-like conditions as the approach of unfavorable weather and shift from their vegetative growth phase to their reproductive phase. An herb such as cilantro will send out a flowering shoot from the center of its basal rosettes in this situation, effectively ending its growth. This is called bolting. Prevent this by giving the herbs a regular supply of water at least once a day and more frequently on hot, dry days.

Feeding for Growth

Herbs need regular feeding to keep them in a perpetual state of growth, especially since you'll be harvesting the leaves often. However, too much feeding can induce excessive growth, which dilutes their flavor. Organic fertilizers are ideal because you want to stay away from chemicals as much as possible when you intend to eat a plant. Fish emulsion, vermicompost, and compost tea are good choices.

Herbs grown indoors can do very well with fertilizers designed for houseplants but feed them at half strength because their root systems are more delicate and more likely to suffer a chemical burn. Newly potted herbs should not be fertilized for two to three weeks, as their roots have to grow well before they can take up nutrients from the soil. Diluted foliar spray of compost tea can give them an initial boost.

Feed garden herbs in late winter or early spring to help them produce healthy new growth. A light top-up once a month is beneficial, but only when they are actively growing.

Harvest Early and Often

Young herbs may look too small and delicate, so the natural instinct is to wait till they attain a good size before starting to harvest them. This is one common mistake that most novice herb gardeners will make at least once. To get a well-branched, bushy plant that provides you with plenty of leaves in the coming months, you should start pinching the growing tip as soon as the plant has three or four sets of leaves.

A "set" simply means all of the leaves that arise from one node. Some plants may have just one leaf at every node, while mint family plants usually have a pair of opposite leaves. You may even find a whorl of leaves at every node in some plants, but each group is still a set, so don't get bogged down in the details. Remember to pinch the growing tip of the main stem with one or two sets of leaves just above a node. The plant will send out new branches from that node so that you will soon have many more leaves to harvest and use.

Pruning

Herbs need a thorough pruning now and then to promote fuller growth. This maintenance prevents them from turning straggly and woody. For most herbs with soft, fleshy stems such as mint, oregano, bee balm, basil, and tarragon, hard pruning should be done whenever they start to show signs of flowering. This shift from the vegetative phase to the reproductive phase will change the herb's flavor and bring about a premature end to the life of your useful plant. You can safely prune herbs two to three times during the growing season, as long as you don't take off more than one-third of the plant at a time. Also, avoid pruning too close to the cold season, as this could interfere with the dormancy period.

For evergreen herbs with woody stems such as rosemary, a spring pruning just as the new growth starts, and maybe another after flowering should be enough. With the bulk of the leafy branches out of the way, you can easily spot any diseases or pest infestations in the plant.

Plan an exclusive herb garden

If you're growing many herbs, starting a garden exclusively for them is a good idea. Even if you may not use up all of your produce, herb gardens are always enjoyable. I love to plant an herb garden very close to my outdoor living spaces as the aromatic oils in the herbs infuse the air with refreshing scents. Many provide natural decorative elements as well, such as silvery foliage or interesting growth patterns—a few even burst with colorful blooms that attract honey bees, hummingbirds, and butterflies. Another benefit is that herbs are easy to grow and generally free of pests and diseases.

Choose a location easily accessible from your house, preferably where the afternoon shadow of your home creates a cooler environment that is ideal for escaping the heat of summer evenings. Prepare the herb beds with plenty of compost incorporated into the soil. Herbs lend themselves well to formal styles like old-fashioned knot gardens and French parterre, or you can plan winding walkways with a few seating areas to create an informal setting.

Companion Planting

If space limitation does not allow the luxury of a dedicated herb garden, you can squeeze herbs into your vegetable beds. Most make good companion plants because they repel pests like aphids, cabbage moths, and tomato worms. Some attract pollinators to the garden and help increase the yield of your vegetable crops. Special care should be taken to pair them up with suitable companions, however. While some herbs, like oregano, tarragon, marjoram, and lovage, make good companions for practically every vegetable, a few, like fennel, don't get along well with any.

Here are a few vegetables and herb companions that will grow well together: chives with carrots; dill and thyme with cabbage; parsley with asparagus; and chervil with radishes. Avoid planting incompatible plants close to one another. For instance, sage goes well with carrots and cabbages but not with cucumbers.

Pesky Pests and Disease

Herbs are less susceptible to pests and diseases than vegetables, but problems do sometimes occur.

Aphids may crowd the tender parts of the plant, while whiteflies and spider mites hide under leaves. Use a strong jet of water to dislodge them as soon as you spot them. Leafhoppers, leaf miners, and caterpillars may partake of your herbs, but they don't usually cause much damage other than leaving slight marks or holes on the leaves. Remember, these half-eaten leaves are still far safer than the pesticide-laden varieties you may purchase from the store.

When determining how to eliminate pests, keep in mind, using chemical pesticides and antimicrobial agents is not part of organic gardening and rarely a good idea for obvious reasons. There is generally a secondary, less harmful option that will remove the pests without spoiling your crop.

Growing herbs in unsuitable conditions is one of the main reasons for many diseases. A few herbs like lemongrass and various mints do well in wet areas, but most other herbs need good drainage. Waterlogging can cause root rot and other fungal infections. Therefore, planting your herbs in raised beds and containers can prevent many problems and keep fast-growing herbs from taking over your main garden.

Hardiness Zones

I have outlined the best United States Department of Agriculture (USDA) hardiness or growing zones for each plant. Garden planting zones provide valuable information about what plants are appropriate for your region.

Although garden zones aren't set in stone, the helpful guidelines prevent guesswork at the garden store, saving gardeners from a world of frustration and disappointment when perennials don't survive winter temperatures.

According to the USDA, hardiness zones are based not on the lowest temperature ever recorded in an area or on temperatures that may occur in the future but on a particular areas average lowest temperatures over a 30-year period.

If you're thinking about starting a garden, it's critical to know your zone before you begin. Why? Because many plants can't tolerate cold weather, while others, such as apples and pears, won't break dormancy and bloom in spring without a chilling period in winter. This explains why you can't grow lemons or avocados outdoors in Minnesota or apples in southern Florida.

While understanding USDA zones is essential, there are other factors that gardeners should think about. For instance, microclimates within a zone are important to consider, as the weather in your garden may be influenced by factors such as elevation or soil drainage. Even a garden space protected by a wall or fence might be slightly warmer than more exposed areas.

Most seed catalogs, greenhouses, and nurseries provide a tag suggesting an appropriate zone range for each plant, such as zone 7 through 9. Most experienced gardeners, however, have learned the hard way not to push the limits too far.

For example, if you live in zone 7, you might want to limit plantings to those suitable for growing in zone 6 or even zone 5. This provides a level of safety in the event of a sudden cold snap and will help you avoid unpleasant surprises if temps fall below average for your region.

Warm weather followed by a sudden plummet in temperatures can also put marginal plants at risk. If you decide to take a chance with plants at the bottom temperatures of your zone, be sure to provide plenty of mulch to protect the roots during the winter.

51 Healing Herbs for Your Backyard Pharmacy

Aloe Vera *(Aloe Vera)*

Hardiness Zone: 8-11

Native to Africa, this plant is popular for its ability to soothe skin conditions and burns. It is also a nutritional powerhouse, full of vitamins and antioxidants. Though many think of this plant as primarily for topical use, Aloe vera barbadensis miller is actually an edible variety that can be enjoyed raw or cooked. Aloe is also a great houseplant for those with limited gardening experience and time, as it thrives even in sub-par conditions.

Healing properties

The leaf of the aloe vera plant is filled with a gel that contains over 75 nutrients, 20 different minerals including calcium, chromium, copper, iron, magnesium, manganese, potassium, phosphorus, sodium, and zinc, 12 vitamins including A, B1, B2, B3, B5, B6, B12, C and E, eight amino acids, and 200 active enzymes. Known as the "burn plant," studies show that aloe vera is highly effective at healing first and second-degree burns. Aloe has anti-inflammatory properties, promotes circulation, and deters bacteria to help reduce the risk of infection.

Starting

The best way to start an aloe vera plant is from "pups" or small aloe plants that are offsets of mature plants. Pups will be attached to the base of the parent plant but will have their own roots and be ready for planting. To remove baby plants from the parent plant, remove the parent plant from its pot. Brush off as much soil as you can from the roots. Gently pull each baby plant from the main plant. Each baby plant must have its own roots. If you have trouble separating the baby from the parent, use a clean, sharp knife to cut it free. Lay the parent plant and pups in a cool, dry place for 48 hours. This gives wounds a chance to heal.

Each baby plant needs its own four-inch or bigger pot. Use cactus compost and gently plant each pup. Tamp the soil down slightly around the baby plants to keep them upright. Wait three days to water and then only water when the soil is completely dry.

According to historical evidence, Alexander the Great and Christopher Columbus both used aloe to treat wounds.

Growing tips

Aloe vera is a succulent plant that does best in dry conditions and is usually grown as a potted houseplant. Plant in cactus potting soil mixes, and be sure that the pot has plenty of drainage holes. Place the pot in a south or west-facing window. Don't worry about fertilization, as it is generally not needed.

Harvesting

Harvest aloe leaves only from mature plants when the tips of the leaves have a rosy hue. Aloes are slow-growing, so be patient and do not over-harvest. Choose a leaf that is large and smooth. Use a clean, sharp knife to cut it as close to the stem as possible. Do not pull the leaf with your hands, as this can damage the plant.

Once you have removed the leaf, it is important to hold the cut side down so that the alonin (a bitter yellow sap) can run out. Carefully wash the leaf and lay it flat on a table. Cut off the serrated edges first. To filet the leaf, start on one side and take as much skin off as you can (it is kind of like filleting a fish). Take the skin off until you see a clear white center. This is the stuff you want to use! Rinse before use.

Storing

To keep aloe leaves fresh and moist, wrap the cut end in tin foil and tie with an elastic band. Place the leaf in a large plastic bag and wrap it tightly. Leaves will stay fresh for about two weeks when stored this way.

Try this

For burns and skin conditions such as stretch marks, dermatitis, and acne, rub liquid from the plant's leaves on clean, dry skin, as needed. Put raw aloe vera meat in your smoothies and use the gel to reduce puffiness in your face.

Anise *(Pimpinella anisum)*

Hardiness Zone: 4-11

Anise, a member of the parsley, carrot, and celery family, is native to Southern Europe and is a Mediterranean herb with a licorice-like aroma and flavor. The medicinal use of this bushy annual herb dates back to as early as 1550 BC, when the ancient Egyptians used it for stomach and oral conditions. Beautiful lacy leaves and white flowers grace this pretty plant. Besides being a popular culinary herb often used in soups, salads, and baked goods, anise seed and oil have a rich history of medicinal use.

Medicinal properties

Anise seed is rich in nutrients and contains calcium, magnesium, and iron, along with antioxidants that may reduce inflammation leading to chronic health conditions. Studies show that the seed may help reduce symptoms of depression and could also help remedy a migraine. Also, anise essential oil has been found to be effective against some fungi and bacteria. Other research indicates that anise seed mimics the effects of estrogen in the body and may reduce symptoms of menopause. As an expectorant, anise is often used to promote a productive cough and remedy digestive woes.

Starting

Start anise plants from seed in biodegradable pots about eight weeks before the last spring frost. Keep seeds at 70 degrees for germination. Sow outdoors once the soil has reached 60 degrees. Use a seed syringe for easy sowing and plant seeds a quarter inch deep at a rate of 12 seeds per foot.

Growing tips

Anise plants reach about 18 inches at maturity. Water young plants twice a week until they reach eight inches tall and then gradually reduce irrigation. Side dress plants with aged compost and apply a nitrogen-rich fertilizer such as blood meal in early June, before flowering. Stake plants as they grow to give them support in blustery weather. Anise will germinate quicker when grown next to coriander so keep that in mind as you select your companion plants.

This herb can also be grown indoors in a bright window or under grow lights but be sure to let the soil dry out completely before watering and use 10-inch pots for container growing.

Do not confuse anise seed with star anise. Although they have a similar name, they are not from the same plant family. Star anise seeds are larger and a dark reddish-brown color, while anise seeds are smaller - more like fennel seeds.

Harvesting

Both the leaves and the seeds can be harvested. Snip fresh leaves at any time using clean, sharp scissors. Seeds require about 100 frost-free days before harvesting. The best time to harvest them is in the fall before the first frost. To harvest anise seeds, you must first cut the flower stems and seed heads, then hang the stalks upside down in a warm, dry, and shady location. Place a paper bag around these heads so that the seeds fall directly into the bag. Once the plant is dry, remove any remaining seeds and put the leftover plant material into the compost.

Storing

Dry anise seed in the oven at 100 degrees F for 15 minutes and store in an airtight container. Leaves can also be dried on a screen in a cool, dry, dark location. Store dried leaves in an airtight container.

Try this

To help relieve gas and bloating, prepare an anise seed tea. Grind two teaspoons of anise seed and add eight ounces of hot water. Steep for 10 minutes, filter, and add local raw honey.

Basil *(Ocimum basilicum)*

Hardiness Zone: 10-11

Basil is one of the most commonly used herbs for cooking and is a staple in many different cuisines, including Italian. This warm-weather plant in the mint family is native to Asia and Africa but will thrive in most climates with proper care. The most common type of basil is **sweet basil**; other types include **purple basil** (less sweet than common basil), **lemon basil** (lemon flavor), and **Thai basil** (licorice flavor). This aromatic and easy-to-grow herb is not only popular as a food enhancer but also as a powerful medicinal plant with a variety of therapeutic compounds.

Medicinal properties

Traditional uses of basil include the treatment of snakebites, colds, and inflammation. Basil contains powerful antioxidants along with calcium and vitamin K. According to research, sweet basil has properties that may protect the skin from the effects of aging. Additional health benefits of sweet basil include the ability to lower blood pressure and blood sugar. Basil essential oils contain potent antimicrobial properties that are effective against various strains of E Coli. Furthermore, there is evidence suggesting that basil can reduce chronic depression and anxiety.

Starting

Start basil seeds indoors six to eight weeks before the last spring frost in biodegradable pots for easy transplant. Plant seeds a quarter-inch deep and seedlings 10 inches apart in the garden.

Growing tips

Basil does best in an area that receives six to eight hours of direct sun. Plant it in well-drained, nutrient-rich soil that's kept moist but never soggy. Use organic fertilizer to help maintain pH levels. If you live in a hot climate, use mulch to retain moisture, as basil hates being totally dry. After seedlings have their first six leaves, prune above the second set to encourage branching. Each time a branch grows six leaves, prune it back to the first set. After six weeks, pinch the center shoot to keep the plant from flowering. Basil grows well indoors in smaller, globe-type containers. Place in a sunny south-facing window or use grow lights.

Harvesting

Once plants are about eight inches tall, begin picking leaves. Harvesting is best in the early morning and should be done regularly during the growing season to encourage growth. Harvest a few individual leaves first, and then cut back individual stems just above a place where side shoots are growing out. This will encourage new growth.

Tomatoes make great companions for basil planted in outdoor gardens. Plus, these plants pair great in the kitchen as well.

Storing

Fresh basil stems keep well for a few days in a jar with tap water placed on the counter. The absolute best way to store fresh basil for future use is to freeze it. Chop up washed basil leaves and add a bit of olive oil. Pulse lightly to coat leaves. Scoop the mixture, place it in silicone ice cube trays, and freeze. Transfer frozen cubes to a freezer bag and use them as needed—one regular-sized cube results in about two tablespoons of fresh basil. Dried basil leaves keep well in a clean jar with a tight-fitting lid. Just be sure not to crumble the leaves to help them retain their valuable essential oils.

Try this

To foster great sleep and beat anxiety, try a cup of sweet basil and lemon tea. Add three large basil leaves and two pieces of washed lemon rind to one cup of hot water. Let it sit for a few minutes, and add some raw honey for sweetener. Sip this tea one hour before bed or anytime you are feeling stressed.

Bee Balm *(Monarda)*

Hardiness Zone: 4-9

Two related plants go by the common name of bee balm. They look similar and have many of the same properties and medicinal uses. *M. fistulosa* is a wild plant native to the eastern U.S. It's called bee balm or wild bergamot, while *M. didyma* is the cultivated version, called scarlet bee balm or just bee balm. Both grow up to four feet tall and three feet wide and have tubular flowers that attract bees and hummingbirds. Scarlet bee balm produces red flowers, while bergamot has lavender blooms. Several Native American tribes used wild bergamot in cooking and drinks and for medicinal uses.

Medicinal properties

Some of those medicinal uses included treating headaches, colds, excessive mucus, bronchial infections, acne, abdominal pains, and eye infections. Early settlers followed this example and also used wild bergamot for infections and headaches. They also added it to tea to mimic the flavor of bergamot orange used in Earl Grey tea. Modern studies have confirmed that compounds in wild bergamot, like thymol, do have antibacterial properties. This explains why it can be used for colds and other infections. It can even help clear up acne.

Starting

Grow either scarlet bee balm or wild bergamot from seed to enjoy its benefits in the garden. It's best to start seeds indoors about eight weeks before the last frost to give the plants a good head start on the growing season. Plant the seeds about a quarter to a half-inch deep.

Growing tips

When the seedlings are ready to go outside, space them 18 inches apart in a sunny spot. They need plenty of space for airflow to reduce the risk of powdery mildew on the leaves. Give bee balm plenty of water throughout the growing season as it prefers evenly moist soil that doesn't dry out entirely. Keep in mind; mulch helps retain moisture in the soil, so add some to your herb garden if you tend to skip a day of watering. If you're worried about the plant growing too vigorously and taking over a bed, let the soil dry out slightly between watering. Deadhead the flowers as they fade to encourage more blooms and divide your bee balm or bergamot plants in spring every few years.

Harvesting

Both the leaves and flowers are edible, but the leaves are most often used for medicinal preparations. Pick leaves at any time, as needed. They have the best flavor before the flowers bloom. If harvesting leaves for storage, take off entire stems to dry. Harvest flowers just after they open.

Storing

Both the leaves and flowers are tasty when used fresh in foods or teas. You can also dry both of them to keep for later use. Lay out the leaves and flowers on a screen in a dry, shady spot or use a dehydrator to speed up the process. Store in an airtight container once completely dry.

Try this

Make a simple bee balm or wild bergamot tea to enjoy the benefits of this tasty plant. Use one teaspoon of dried, crumbled leaves in a cup of boiling water. Let it steep for about five minutes and strain through a fine sieve. The taste is similar to Earl Grey, but it can be a little strong. You may want to experiment with the number of leaves or try adding other herbs to find your perfect blend.

Broadleaf plantain *(Plantago major)*

Hardiness Zone: 3-9

Broadleaf plantain, native to Europe and temperate regions in Asia, is a compact, perennial, flowering herb with egg-shaped waxy leaves and visible veins. Also known as birdseed, healing blade, and hen plant, broadleaf plantain is one of 34 Plantago species found worldwide - all of which are edible and medicinal. Small brown seed pods contain between four to 20 seeds each. When these pods are mature, they split and scatter seeds on the ground, where they can last up to 60 years in the soil.

Medicinal properties

Broadleaf plantain leaves are loaded with calcium and other minerals as well as vitamins like vitamin K. The tender leaves are fantastic eaten raw in a salad, but if they aren't fresh, you can cook them or make a plantain tea. Broadleaf plantain can soothe bug bites, stings, and other skin conditions and is known as nature's "band-aid", meaning it can inhibit bacteria growth and relieve pain and inflammation. Sipping on this herb in tea is also a great way to alleviate digestive ailments, including IBS and other inflammatory problems in the gastrointestinal tract.

Starting

For indoor seed starting, place seeds in the freezer for two weeks. Start seeds outdoors six to eight weeks before the last expected spring frost. After spreading the seed, simply tamp the soil with the back of a hoe, and spread a little mulch to prevent weed growth and lock in moisture. Keep the soil moist until seeds germinate and grow a bit. After it is established, plantain is easy to transplant if you have some that you would like to dig up and relocate or share with a friend.

Growing tips

Once plantain plants are started, there's no need to turn the soil; this herb can loosen hard, compacted soils on its own. As it's quite hardy, it can be walked on over and over, so it's great for growing on pathways and will flourish in a variety of soil pH and climates. Very little maintenance is required once plantain is established.

Harvesting

Harvest leaves any time during the growing season, including before, during, and after flowering. The fresh inner leaves are the tastiest; snip them off close to the stem using clean, sharp scissors. Early-season harvests work best for tinctures, but you can harvest seeds later in the season once seed pods rattle inside and the pod has turned brown. Run your hand up dried stalks and pull off seeds, placing them in a plastic bag. Sift them through a fine strainer and blow on them gently to remove any leftover husks. If using the roots, it is best to harvest in the fall as this is when the plant's energy is directed downward. Gently pull up the plant and gather the roots.

Don't worry about harvesting too often. Broadleaf plantain is a hardy, prolific plant that will keep coming back no matter how much you take!

Storing

This plant is best used fresh from the garden, but dried leaves are useful for teas and herbal remedies. Dehydrate at 95 degrees F in the oven for best results and store dried leaves in a clean jar with a lid.

Try This

Make a plantain tincture by combining one part fresh leaves with two parts vodka. Place mixture in a jar with a lid and shake well, then store it in a dark place for six weeks and strain. It will keep for up to a year when stored in an airtight container. Keep it in your bathroom and pour some on a clean cotton pad to dab on acne spots twice a day as needed.

Calendula *(Calendula officianalis)*

Hardiness Zone: 3–10

Calendula, also known as pot marigold, belongs to the same family as daisies and chrysanthemums, not common marigolds. Native to southern Europe and the Mediterranean, calendula has been cultivated for centuries, and the leaves and flowers are both used in medicine and food. Most people grow it as an annual, but it is a perennial in warmer climates. Calendula produces bright yellow and orange daisy-like flowers that bloom for a long time until the first frost of the season.

Medicinal properties

The medicinal uses of calendula come from the petals. Not many people consume them, but ointments, washes, and tinctures made from the flowers have several topical benefits. These preparations may help wounds heal faster by bringing more blood to the cut, scrape, or burn. They can also be used to relieve hemorrhoids, dermatitis, and other types of skin inflammation. Ear drops with calendula may even help treat ear infections.

Starting

Calendula is easy to start from seed. Sow seeds just before the last expected frost in fertile, well-drained soil. Be sure to select a location that receives full sun. Space seeds about six inches apart and cover with a quarter to a half-inch of soil. You can keep sowing seeds through early summer to get continuous blooms well into the fall. Grow in beds or containers indoors or outside.

Growing tips

Calendula needs regular watering while the roots establish, but once mature, it does better with occasional watering as it does not like to sit in soggy soil. Use a balanced fertilizer once a month for container plants and none for those in beds with good soil; calendula is not a heavy feeder, so don't over-fertilize. Keep pinching back young calendula plants as they grow to encourage a bushier, fuller shape and avoid leggy, spindly plants. Deadhead spent flowers for more blooms.

Harvesting

Harvest calendula flowers when they are fully open and mature in the late morning after the dew has dried. Pinch or cut the flower heads off right where they meet the top of the stem. You can pick leaves for culinary uses at any time as the plant grows.

Storing

You can use the flowers and leaves fresh right after picking them. To keep a harvest longer, dry the flowers by spreading them out on drying racks, a screen, or a clean cloth. If you have a humid climate, air drying may not be feasible. In that case, try a food dehydrator set on its lowest setting. Store dried flowers or petals in an airtight container out of the light. Remember to double-check flowers after dehydrating as they must be completely dry to store without the risk of rotting.

Try this

Prepare a calendula oil to treat skin issues. Choose an oil for your skin type - grapeseed, jojoba, and sweet almond are all good options. Add dried calendula flowers to a glass jar until it is about three-quarters full. Fill the rest of the jar with the oil. Let it sit in a sunny, warm spot for about three weeks. Strain the flowers and keep the oil, using it on your skin as needed.

Catnip *(Nepeta cataria)*

Hardiness Zone: 3-9

Catnip is an herb native to southwest Asia and much of Europe. It belongs to the same family as mint and contains an essential oil that many cats love: nepetalactone. Though it seems like every cat is obsessed with catnip, this sensitivity is hereditary and is not expressed until a cat is about six months old. For cats that are affected, catnip triggers certain behaviors such as drooling, rolling around, vocalizing, and playing energetically.

Catnip has naturalized in many parts of the world, so you may see it growing wild in fields or along roads. It grows two to three feet tall, has leaves similar to mint, and produces spikes of small, white flowers.

Medicinal properties

While cats enjoy catnip, it has no known therapeutic benefits for them. For humans, however, catnip has some practical and medicinal uses. Catnip tea has long been used as a diuretic, an indigestion cure, and as a remedy for coughing, arthritis, fever, and infections. While not many studies exist to prove the benefits of catnip, researchers have found that nepetalactone is similar to the essential oil in valerian, known for inducing relaxation.

Starting

Catnip transplants are easy to find in garden centers, but you can also grow this herb from seed. Put the seeds in a freezer overnight and soak them in warm water for about 24 hours. They are then ready to plant in the soil at higher germination rates. Start seeds indoors in a seed tray and move transplants outdoors or into containers after the risk of frost has passed.

Growing Tips

Give your growing catnip plants about 18 to 24 inches of space to spread out and plenty of direct sunlight. They need soil that drains sufficiently, but it doesn't need to be very fertile. Keep in mind; like mint, catnip will take over garden beds. It's best grown in containers unless you want to have a whole bed designated for catnip. You can even grow it indoors in pots by a sunny window if you want a cat-friendly indoor herb for your furry friend to enjoy. Pinch the stems as they grow to encourage a full shape. Water regularly and let the soil dry out between watering.

Harvesting

The best way to harvest catnip is to cut down the entire plant or entire stems. Do this after the plant has flowered. You can hang the whole plant or stems upside down to dry. Crumble the dried leaves for storage.

Catnip and catmint are related but not the same plant. Catmint is *Nepeta mussinii*. The flowers are lavender colored, and the plant looks a little less weedy than catnip. You can use catmint leaves as you would mint in the kitchen.

Storing

Only store the plant and leaves when completely dry. Any moisture can lead to rotting. Keep the leaves in an airtight container and store them in a dark, dry spot in the house.

Try this

Cats will be thrilled with a sprinkling of crushed, dried catnip on their toys. For human consumption, make a simple tea by mixing two teaspoons of crushed leaves with one cup of boiling water. Steep for 10 to 15 minutes.

Cayenne *(Capsicum annuum)*

Hardiness Zone: 9-11

Cayenne is a hot chili pepper native to South America. Though not the hottest of the peppers, it is versatile in the kitchen and is one of the most commonly used peppers. Cayenne pepper plants can grow up to four feet tall and two feet wide, with attractive dark green leaves and multi-colored peppers. This is a pretty, ornamental plant that thrives in subtropical and tropical gardens, but most people grow it to use the peppers in the kitchen.

Medicinal properties

Cayenne pepper adds a tasty spice to many dishes, but it also has medicinal properties and health benefits. Capsaicin is the active ingredient in hot peppers. Studies have found that capsaicin boosts metabolism, causing people to burn more calories and experience a reduced appetite. There is also evidence that capsaicin lowers blood pressure and may benefit digestive health. Though results are not definitive, some studies have shown that capsaicin may reduce cancer risk, slow cancer cell growth, and even kill cancer cells. You may notice that different sore muscle balms contain capsaicin, which can help relieve pain.

Starting

If you live in the right climate, grow cayenne outdoors year-round. In colder climates, you can grow it as an annual or indoors in containers. In most areas, you'll need to start seeds in containers inside. In zones nine and higher, you can start them outside in beds a couple of weeks before the last frost, if applicable.

Growing tips

If growing outside as an annual, take your indoor seedlings out six to eight weeks after starting the seeds. Provide them with a spot that has well-drained soil and plenty of sun. Indoors, keep them by a sunny window, and be sure to keep them warm. Cayenne is picky about water. Keep the soil at a medium moisture level. The plants won't tolerate soggy soil, but they also don't like dry soil. Avoid fertilizer with too much nitrogen, which will stunt pepper growth.

Harvesting

Cayenne peppers are ready to harvest when they have ripened to the right color. This depends on the variety. They start green and then ripen to red, orange, yellow, or even white. Use shears to pick peppers, as picking them by hand can damage the plant. Continue harvesting as the peppers ripen.

Storing

Use fresh peppers in the kitchen within a week or so. To keep peppers longer, dry them. Use a food dehydrator or your oven at the lowest temperature. It should take two to three hours to dry them completely. Turn them a few times as they dry. Store the dried peppers in airtight containers. To save the seeds, cut them from the fresh peppers and lay them out on a paper towel to dry. Store in a jar or plastic bag.

Try this

Combine cayenne pepper with apple cider vinegar and hot water for a tea that will clear your sinuses.

Chamomile *(Matricaria recutita)*

Hardiness Zone: 5-9

Who doesn't love chamomile tea? It's one of the most popular herbal teas, frequently used to help promote better sleep and a sense of calmness. It can also help remedy digestive ailments and contains a powerful antioxidant to reduce inflammation that can lead to illness and disease. German chamomile will add a beautiful pop of white to any kitchen herb garden and is a practical plant to have on hand.

Medicinal properties

Compounds in chamomile are soothing and anti-inflammatory, and it is useful for relieving minor aches and pains. A study published in *Molecular Medicine Report* found that chamomile can effectively reduce the pain from hemorrhoids, arthritis, ulcers, menstrual cramps, and wounds. Along with the above-listed conditions, chamomile has also been linked to lowered cholesterol, reduced risk of blood clotting, and soothed stomach pain. Aside from its internal benefits, chamomile may help to improve many types of skin conditions when applied externally. Potential uses for this herb include the treatment of acne, eczema, psoriasis, and other types of skin inflammation.

There are two types of chamomile, so it is vital to understand what you are planting. German chamomile produces long, flimsy stems and tons of delicate white flowers that look very similar to daisies. This is the variety most frequently used for tea and tinctures since it produces an abundance of blooms. Roman chamomile is usually used as a fast-spreading ground cover to fill in holes in your garden and provide a nice, fragrant element. Both varieties are technically annuals but will reseed and spread with vigor, coming back each year in abundance. Keep that in mind before you choose a planting spot.

Starting

Start seeds indoors under a grow light about six to eight weeks before your last expected frost date. Lightly tamp down the seeds into your growing medium and mist with water to avoid disturbing the seeds. Once all danger of frost has passed, transplant seedlings to the garden, leaving a space of about 8 to 12 inches between plants.

Growing tips

Chamomile thrives outdoors, but it also grows well indoors in a pot. Since it requires only four hours of sunlight per day, it will do well indoors as long as it has a spot by a south-facing window. Keep the soil moist but not overly wet, watering only about once per week.

Once established, this pretty plant requires very little care. It's drought-tolerant and only needs water during times of prolonged dryness. Water seedlings frequently until they put down roots and then only occasionally, as it is best to let the roots dry out slightly between waterings. In just a few weeks, you should see your first blooms developing on the spindly, green stems. Since chamomile is so hardy, it doesn't require any fertilizer and will grow strong and tall with minimal care. Plus, it doesn't attract many pests or diseases, making it an excellent "leave it and forget it" herb.

Harvesting

Once the flower petals begin to curl downward, cut off the flowers and lay them on a mesh surface to dry. Chamomile leaves tend to be bitter and unappealing, so once you cut off the flowers, trim the stalks to about six inches above the ground. Leave the spent stalks on the ground, as they will decompose quickly and add essential nutrients back into the soil. Though you can use fresh flowers for tea, drying this useful herb will allow it to last longer, and you won't need as many flowers since the flavor will be more concentrated. Keep the flowers spread out for about a week in a cool, dry place and then store in a glass jar or airtight bag.

Storing

The best way to preserve chamomile flowers for future use is to use a food dehydrator set on the lowest setting for about 12 to 18 hours. Another interesting way to preserve chamomile is to freeze it. Harvest flowers and wrap them in aluminum foil. Store the package in the coolest part of your freezer, all the way in the back. Frozen flowers keep for about six months or longer if not subject to thawing and refreezing.

Try this

One of the best ways to reap all of the fantastic benefits of chamomile is to brew a lovely, aromatic cup of relaxing tea. Measure out about two tablespoons of dried flowers for every eight-ounce cup of tea you wish to make. Boil water and pour it over the flowers, letting it steep for about five minutes. Then strain through a fine tea sieve. Feel free to add any of your favorite herbs, such as mint, to mix up the flavor slightly. You can also use local raw honey for sweetener, lemon for a bit of zing, or a little coconut creamer for a wonderful nighttime drink.

Chickweed *(Stellaria media)*

Hardiness Zone: 4-11

Common chickweed is a plant native to Europe, but it has become naturalized throughout the U.S. and other areas of the world. It tends to grow in moist soils in full sun or partial shade and is incredibly hardy, which is why some consider it a weed when it pops up in their lawn. Chickweed is edible and has been used for centuries in folk remedies for a range of medical issues. Common chickweed grows low to the ground and has a stringy appearance. The oval leaves have a pointed tip, and the flowers are small, white, and daisy-like. A unique identifying characteristic is a thin line of fine hairs along the stems.

Medicinal properties

Use chickweed leaves any way you would use lettuce or baby greens. They have a pleasant, delicate flavor when eaten raw and contain nutrients like vitamin C and flavonoids. Folk remedies using chickweed have found some support in modern research. When consumed as a food or juice, chickweed supports healthy digestion and weight, possibly because it slows the absorption of fats and carbohydrates in the body. Chickweed may also be useful as an expectorant when you have a cold, and it reduces inflammation and may help heal wounds.

Starting

Chickweed is incredibly easy to grow from seed. To start from seed, plant about three seeds per inch in a starter tray and cover with a quarter-inch of soil. Thin the seedlings as they grow to about five inches between each plant. Or, if you have some in your lawn or garden, you can dedicate an area to growing it or dig it up and plant it in containers indoors or out.

Growing tips

Start chickweed inside or directly in a bed or container outdoors in autumn or late winter. This is a winter annual, so don't wait until spring to plant. It grows best in rich soil with added compost that drains but also retains some moisture. Keep chickweed well-watered but not soggy. It will do best in a spot with a bit of shade as well. Use mulch in sunnier areas to help keep the soil moist. Chickweed will grow well without any fertilizer.

Harvesting

To harvest chickweed, cut off the top sections of stems as you need them. Don't remove the entire plant if you want it to propagate itself for next year. You can use the stems, leaves, and flowers fresh as you harvest them. Avoid harvesting the lower parts of stems, however, as these can be tough and unpalatable.

Storing

Chickweed is best used fresh, although you can air dry it if you want to store the plant material for medicinal uses later. Let the plants dry out thoroughly before storing them in an airtight container. For fresh chickweed, keep it no longer than a few days in the vegetable drawer of your refrigerator.

Try this

Make chickweed-infused oil to soothe irritated, inflamed skin. Combine about two cups of leaves with one cup of coconut oil. Process in a blender and warm it on the stove in a double boiler to infuse. Let it sit for several hours, and then rewarm and strain out the leaves once the oil is green. When it cools and hardens, you'll have a salve.

Chives *(Allium schoenoprasum)*

Hardiness Zone: 3-9

A perennial member of the onion family, chives are not only beautiful and a versatile culinary herb, but they also contain several therapeutic properties. Chives are one of the first plants to pop up after winter and, once established, will happily come back year after year. With a super long growing season, chives even grow year-round in some mild climates. In addition to tasty green stems, pink edible blossoms bloom throughout spring and make a beautiful addition to salads and even baked goods!

Medicinal properties

Chives are rich in vitamins C and K and are a particularly good source of vitamin A, with 145 percent of the recommended daily allowance (RDA) in just half a cup. This popular herb contains lutein and zeaxanthin, which are carotenoids that help prevent age-related macular degeneration in the eyes. Vitamin C helps keep the immune system strong, while vitamin K improves bone health. Studies show that diallyl trisulfide found in chives is a possible anticancer agent. Further studies demonstrate the importance of sulfur compounds in chives and other allium vegetables in decreasing the bioactivation of carcinogens. Traditionally, chives were also used to ease digestive woes and as a remedy for intestinal parasites.

Starting

For spring planting, start seeds indoors six weeks before the last average frost date. Sow six seeds per cell in a 72-cell plug tray. Once chives reach two inches tall, thin them to the six strongest seedlings per cell. Either continue to grow them indoors or transplant them outside once they are six inches tall.

You can also direct sow as soon as the soil is workable and at least 60 degrees F. Sow seeds two inches apart and a quarter inch deep. Once seedlings emerge, thin so that plants are four inches apart. Chives prefer moist and fertile soil that drains well and will do best in full sun or light shade.

Growing tips

Chives can grow just about anywhere, including indoors. Keep them in the kitchen, and you'll have an easy-to-grab supply. Choose a sunny south-facing window that gets six to eight hours of full sunlight each day, rotating your containers if the chives begin to reach toward the light. Mist them every day with a spray bottle to prevent low humidity, and water the plants whenever the

Chives are a welcome plant in any garden space. They attract pollinators and repel some of the most unwanted pests, keeping other plants safe due to their strong onion scent.

soil's surface is dry to the touch. Minimal care is needed indoors and outdoors once plants are established. After the flowers bloom, be sure to remove them so that the seeds do not spread. Divide plants every three years in clumps containing at least 10 small bulbs.

Harvesting

Begin harvesting 30 days after transplanting or 60 days after seeding. Cut the stems to the base when harvesting - at about two inches from the soil. Harvest new plants three or four times in the first year and monthly after that.

Storing

Wrap fresh chives in a paper towel and place them in a plastic bag in the fridge. They will generally keep for about one week. Freeze chives whole in bundles in a plastic freezer bag, snip off what you need, and reseal the bag.

Try this

Freeze whole chive flowers into individual ice cubes and enjoy them in your favorite summer drinks.

Chrysanthemum *(Chrysanthemum spp.)*

Hardiness Zone: 6-9

Chrysanthemums, also known as mums, are popular flowers to grow in gardens. Most associated with fall blooms, the mums most often sold in garden centers are decorative and treated as annuals. Other types are hardy perennials planted in spring. Mums come in various flower shapes and colors, from small button-like blooms to large, spidery flowers. The cultivation of chrysanthemum dates back a few thousand years to China, where it has long been used as a health tonic for various ailments.

Medicinal properties

In traditional Chinese medicine, chrysanthemum is considered a cooling herb, used to clear heat, purify the blood, calm the liver, soothe the nervous system, and rejuvenate the body and mind. Practitioners use chrysanthemum tea for hyperthyroidism, inflammation, high blood pressure, respiratory illnesses, and anxiety. Some modern research has found medicinal properties in chrysanthemum that back up its use in ancient medicine. Some of the compounds found in mums reduce inflammation. There is also some evidence that this plant supports osteoporosis treatment and effectively boosts liver health and good eyesight.

The two types of chrysanthemum used to make tea and other medicinal preparations are *C. morifolium* and *C. indicum*.

Starting

Start seeds for mums indoors about eight weeks before the last date for a spring frost. It will take at least 16 weeks from seed-starting to flowering, so beginning seeds indoors provides a head start. Mum seeds are tiny, so scatter in pinches in a growing tray and cover lightly with soil.

Growing tips

Plant mums outside when they are a few inches tall and there is no danger of frost. Give them 18 to 36 inches of space and provide a spot in full sun. The soil should drain well but stay reliably and evenly moist. Chrysanthemums do best with a monthly balanced fertilizer (10-10-10). Stop adding fertilizer once the flower buds appear. Pinch off the top two or three leaves from stems as they develop to encourage bushy growth. Mums do well in beds and containers. You can also grow them indoors as long as they get plenty of light.

Harvesting

Pick chrysanthemum flowers just as they begin to bloom and before they are fully open. Use shears or scissors to snip them off just at the top of the stem.

Storing

Try using fresh flowers blanched and added to salads and stir-fries. Chrysanthemum flowers for medicinal preparations are best used dried, so lay out harvested blooms in a dry, shaded spot. Let them dry completely before storing and keep them in an airtight jar in a cool location.

Try this

Make a healing cup of chrysanthemum tea with dried flowers. Use three to six flowers per eight ounces of water. Boil the water and then let it cool to about 100 degrees Fahrenheit. Steep the flowers for five to 10 minutes.

Cilantro *(Coriandrum sativum L)*

Hardiness Zone: 3-10

Cilantro is one of the oldest spices in the world. It is native to the Middle East and the Mediterranean region, and its culinary and medicinal uses have been traced back to 5000 B.C.E. This herb is a true superfood and medicinal powerhouse, with countless ways to use it to enhance the taste and nutrition of your food. Frequently used in Mexican, Caribbean, and Asian cooking, this herb is best added toward the end of cooking, which helps maintain its fresh flavor.

Medicinal properties

Cilantro leaves are rich in vitamins, including vitamins A, C, and K. The volatile oils found in this plant and its seeds are high in flavonoid antioxidants kaempferol and quercetin, along with phenolic acids. Cilantro leaves and seeds help combat pain and chronic inflammation and may ease anxiety. Antioxidants and essential oils found in cilantro help support cardiovascular health and tackle several types of bacteria, including Listeria monocytogenes and Candida albicans - common yeast infection. Extracts from the cilantro plant may even help reduce sun damage to the skin.

Starting

For outdoor gardens, cilantro does not require an indoor start. It grows quickly and develops a taproot, making it difficult to transplant. Prepare the soil with organic matter and sow seeds a half-inch deep in late spring or early summer—thin seedlings to six inches apart once they have a few leaves. For cilantro all season long, sow seeds every two weeks.

For indoor growing, fill an eight-inch container with potting soil an inch or two from the top, and then press the seeds down. Water until the soil is moist but not soggy. Cover it up using plastic wrap, securing it with rubber bands, and place it in a sunny location. Once the seeds have germinated, which usually only takes a few days, remove the plastic wrap. Water daily.

Growing tips

Water seedlings daily. Provide a water-soluble fertilizer when plants reach about two inches tall unless growing for seeds. Pinch back young plants when they reach an inch or so to promote bushier growth. Cutting off flower heads redirects energy to the leaves and not flower production. Of course, if you want the coriander seeds, you must let the plant flower and go to seed. Cilantro tends to bolt quickly in hot weather and is a fall crop in some locations. Once cilantro is established, it does not need much water, so be careful not to overwater.

In the United States, cilantro refers to the plant's leaves, and coriander refers to its seeds. In other parts of the world, the plant is known as coriander and its seeds as coriander seeds.

Harvesting

Harvest leaves any time using clean, sharp scissors. For seeds, harvest on a dry day and cut the top part of the stems when the seedpods start to turn brown and crack when pressed. The key is to harvest seeds before the plants release them into your garden. Place cut stems in a paper bag and put it in a cool, dark place with good ventilation. Roll and shake pods to release the seeds.

Storing

Store dried seeds in a jar with a lid placed in a dark location. Place freshly harvested leaves in a plastic freezer bag and store them in the freezer.

Try this

Make delicious herbal vinegar by adding 12 sprigs of fresh cilantro, three hot chili peppers, and six cloves of peeled and halved garlic to six cups of distilled white vinegar. Store vinegar in a cool, dark place for three weeks and strain. Pour into individual bottles and add fresh sprigs of cilantro and garlic cloves.

Comfrey *(Symphytum officinale)*

Hardiness Zone: 4-8

Comfrey, a perennial herb - often identified as a weed - native
to the ditches and riverbanks of Europe, has long been used in
traditional medicine. Records dating back as far as the Middle Ages
reference using comfrey for a wide range of conditions. Comfrey has
slender, long leaves and black-skinned roots that produce clusters of
blue, purple, and white flowers. There is some evidence that comfrey
should not be ingested due to its potentially toxic impacts on the
liver. Even so, the topical use of comfrey is recognized as a valuable
herbal remedy.

Medicinal properties

Comfrey is used to speed up the healing process of wounds, likely due to its high calcium and vitamin C concentrations. The plant is loaded with antioxidants, making it an excellent option for skin problems and insect bites. Herbalists, naturopaths, and functional practitioners often use comfrey as their "go-to" natural remedy for eczema, psoriasis, and even acne. Rubbing comfrey leaf extract on mosquito bites, spider, or tick bites soothes itching, reduces inflammation, and helps keep infection at bay.

Additionally, comfrey has received a great deal of attention in the scientific community regarding bone and joint injuries and chronic disorders. Research shows that comfrey's potent anti-inflammatory, analgesic, and tissue regeneration properties can reduce pain associated with sprains while increasing flexibility.

Starting

The best way to start comfrey is from a live root cutting or transplant. This is much easier than starting from seed.

Growing tips

Comfrey can be grown almost anywhere, indoors or out. This hardy plant can withstand temperatures as low as 40 degrees below zero and as high as 120 degrees Fahrenheit. While it prefers soil with a pH of 6.0 to 7.0, it tends to adapt well to nearly any environment, dry or wet, full sun or partial shade. Simply plant it, sit back to watch it grow, and then reap the rewards.

Harvesting

Because comfrey is such a quick grower, leaves can be harvested up to four times a year, with the first cutting by mid-spring. Reserve harvesting for second-year plants, however, as it is best to give it some time to get established. Cut back all the leaves to about two inches above the soil. If you want individual leaves only, wait to harvest until they reach the size of your hand. Stop cutting in early fall so that plants can build up winter reserves.

Comfrey leaves have tiny prickly hairs on stems and leaves that may cause skin irritation. Wear gloves and a long-sleeved shirt when harvesting.

Storing

Dry comfrey leaves by stringing them up on a thread and placing them in a warm, sunny place away from pests. You can also use a food dehydrator. Ensure that leaves are crumbly before using them to make oil or other remedies. Store dried leaves in a glass jar with a lid in a dark place.

Try this

Make a poultice to help reduce inflammation and soothe pain by combining four cups of chopped leaves and stems with a quarter cup of almond oil. Wrap this paste in a cotton cloth, freeze it, and apply it to problem areas, leaving it for 30 or more minutes to relieve pain and swelling.

Dandelion *(Taraxacum officinale)*

Hardiness Zone: 3-9

Dandelion, considered a weed by so many, is incredibly nutritious and has several medicinal and health benefits. There's no mistaking the sunny yellow blooms that dot lawns throughout the summer. The leaf of the dandelion is highly toothed, which is where the name originated. In French, 'dent de lion' means tooth of the lion. Dandelions are native to Asia and Europe, but they have become established in many parts of the world. People have long used all parts of the dandelion to make wine, a coffee-like drink, food, and medicines.

Medicinal properties

Dandelion flowers, leaves, and roots are edible and nutritious. The greens, in particular, are rich in vitamins A, C, and K, iron, magnesium, potassium, and calcium. The root has a lot of fiber that supports a healthy bacterial ecosystem in the gut, while all parts contain significant amounts of antioxidants.

Historical medical uses for dandelion included treating fever, liver diseases, diarrhea, boils, heartburn, and more. Today, studies have shown dandelion can be effective for reducing inflammation, controlling blood sugar, reducing cholesterol, lowering blood pressure, promoting liver health, and aiding digestion.

Starting

While most people have unwanted dandelions, there are good reasons to cultivate them. It allows you to control the timing and harvest, and you don't have to worry about contaminating lawn treatments like pesticides and herbicides. Sow seeds outside beginning in early spring and continue sowing every couple of weeks through summer for a constant harvest. You can also start seeds indoors and grow dandelions in containers.

Growing tips

Dandelion care is minimal. They thrive in sunlight but will tolerate some shade. They are not picky about soil either; however, they do prefer consistent soil moisture, so keep your dandelions watered regularly and don't let the soil dry out all the way. There is no need to fertilize.

Harvesting

Dandelion leaves and flowers are best when young and tender. Pull the entire plant or harvest leaves and flowers as you need them. You can harvest and use the roots at any time. Also, try picking the flower buds. They have a unique flavor and can be enjoyed raw.

Storing

Eat fresh greens and flowers immediately for the best results. You can store the flowers in water and the greens in the vegetable crisper for a few days. If using the leaves for medicinal preparations, let them dry entirely and store them in an airtight container. Clean and cut roots into small pieces. Dry them in a low-temperature oven or food dehydrator.

Try this

Enjoy the benefits of dandelion in a cup of coffee. Roast the roots in a 300-degree oven for 10 to 15 minutes. Steep a tablespoon of the root pieces in boiling water for ten minutes. You'll get a drink that looks like coffee. The taste is similar but totally unique. You can also add dandelion root to coffee or steep it with spices, like cinnamon and cardamom, for a chai-like tisane.

Dill *(Anethum graveolens)*

Hardiness Zone: 2-11

Often called dill weed, the leaves of dill plants add a flavorful touch to salads, meats, sauces, and vegetables, while dill seed is often used in bread, pickles, coleslaw, and sauerkraut. Dill is a self-seeding annual herb with tiny greenish-yellow flowers that bloom on flat-topped clusters. Planting dill in your garden ensures that you will have plenty of friendly pollinators like butterflies and bees come to visit. This pretty plant is grown as an annual and tolerates both cold and hot temperatures well. Although dill is well-known as a culinary spice, it has impressive nutritional and medicinal value.

Medicinal properties

Dill is loaded with vitamins, including fat-soluble vitamin A that is useful for healthy vision, immune function, skin, and reproductive health. It also contains vitamin C, a vital antioxidant that helps the body keep infection at bay and reduces chronic inflammation that leads to dangerous conditions like heart disease, rheumatoid arthritis, and even cancer.

Dill has been found to help lower blood sugar and is often used as a breath freshener and colic reliever. Dill is also widely recognized for its antimicrobial properties. This feathery garden beauty is a good source of fiber, folate, calcium, riboflavin, manganese, and iron. For centuries, dill has been used in traditional Asian and Ayurvedic medicine for various medical purposes, including cough, bronchitis, insomnia, fever, colds, and loss of appetite.

Starting

Sow dill seeds directly into your garden after the threat of spring frost has passed and the soil temperature is between 60 and 70 degrees F. Germination will happen in 10 to 14 days. For a continual supply of dill all season long, plant seeds every two weeks until mid-summer. Sow seeds about a quarter inch deep and 18 inches apart in well-draining soil amended with rich organic matter.

Growing tips

Plant dill next to cabbage and onions in the garden but keep it away from carrots. Shelter dill from strong winds as it can blow over easily. During the growing season, water often and don't let it dry out excessively, as dill isn't drought tolerant. For a more extended harvest, pick off any blooms you notice before they can open. You can grow dill indoors, but it must be in a sunny window or under grow lights.

Harvesting

When dill has four to five leaves, start harvesting. Harvest older leaves first by pinching them off or cutting them with clean, sharp pruning scissors. If you have a lot of plants to harvest, cut entire stalks to save time.

Harvest in the morning after dew has evaporated when it is at its peak freshness. To harvest seeds, let a few of your plants go to seed instead of pinching off blooms. Once flowers fade, the seeds will begin to form at the top of the star-shaped flower stems. Allow the seeds to dry on the plant, clip the entire plant head, and put it in a paper bag. Most seeds will fall off into the bag; pick off those that don't.

Storing

If you plan on using the dill within a week, place the stems in a jar filled with water just like you would with fresh flowers. You can also freeze dill by putting the leaves in a blender and finely chopping them. Add just enough water to make a paste, spoon the paste into ice cube trays, and freeze. Once frozen, transfer cubes to a plastic bag and place them in the freezer. Use as needed. If storing seeds, be sure to dry them and keep them in an airtight glass container in a cool location.

Try this

Add two teaspoons of bruised dill seeds to a cup of hot water to make dill tea. Steep for 10 minutes before straining through a fine sieve. Drink to ease an upset stomach.

Echinacea *(Echinacea purpurea)*

Hardiness Zone: 5-8

Echinacea is the name of a group of perennial flowering plants in the daisy family. Not only is echinacea - or purple coneflower - incredibly beautiful, it is quite useful as an herbal remedy as well. Plus, it is a perfect addition to the garden if you want to attract pollinators to your yard. While all parts of the plant, including the roots and seeds, are safe for human consumption, the flowers are primarily used in various tinctures and teas for medicinal use.

Medicinal properties

Echinacea contains antioxidants, including flavonoids, rosmarinic acid, and cichoric acid, that help the body defend against oxidative stress caused by free radicals. Human studies support the use of echinacea for immune support and show that it can even speed up recovery from the common cold by stimulating the immune system to work faster and more efficiently. This pretty herb may also reduce chronic inflammation, decrease feelings of anxiety, and help lower blood sugar levels. Antibacterial and anti-inflammatory properties suppress the growth of Propionibacterium, a common cause of acne. Echinacea extract helps hydrate the skin, prevent wrinkles, improve eczema symptoms, and repair the outer layer of the skin. Test-tube studies show that echinacea extracts may even kill human cancer cells.

Starting

Because coneflowers started from seed can take several years to produce flowers, it is best to start with a young plant or division. To ensure beautiful blooms, plant your coneflowers in an area with well-draining soil and plenty of sunlight. Although they can do well in poor soil, echinacea prefers rich, fertile soil and organic matter.

Growing tips

Water echinacea regularly until it's well-established. After this, it rarely needs watering, and overwatering is usually a bigger concern. Apply a thin layer of compost and a layer of mulch around plants for moisture retention. To delay blooming until spring, cut coneflowers back by a foot when plants come into bloom. This will also encourage a more compact growth habit.

Keep coneflower plants in pots through the winter. Prune them back to soil level in the late fall and move to an area where they will get indirect light and temperatures between 40 to 50 degrees F. Water lightly when the top three inches of soil becomes dry. Move plants to a brighter and warmer location, about 60 to 70 degrees F, in the spring to prepare for outdoor weather again.

Apply additional mulch in the fall in cooler regions. Cut plants back in the winter or early spring before new growth starts. Coneflowers also grow well in containers, but make sure that they are deep enough for the plant's taproot - at least two gallons. Ensure there are drainage holes and water deeply when soil is dry to the touch. Provide a balanced fertilizer every two weeks during the growing season and deadhead to keep plants in bloom longer.

Harvesting

Harvest leaves and buds in the second year or immediately if you decide to plant established coneflowers. Cut the stem above the lowest set of leaves, strip the leaves and flower buds from the stem, and lay them out flat. For roots, only harvest from three-year-old plants and older. Use a shovel or garden fork to lift the roots from the ground gently. Take off pieces of the root ball and place the plant back into the ground.

Storing

Dry plant leaves and buds by laying them out on a screen in a well-ventilated area away from direct sunlight; roots can be dried in the same way after washing but will need about two weeks to dry fully. Store any dried pieces in an airtight container in a dark, cool location such as a pantry.

Try this

Enjoy echinacea tea by simmering half a cup of fresh or a quarter cup of dried leaves, roots, and flowers in one cup of filtered water for about 15 minutes. Strain and add raw honey to taste.

Feverfew *(Tanacetum parthenium)*

Hardiness Zone: 5-9

Native to Asia Minor and the Balkans, feverfew, related to the daisy, is grown throughout the world and commonly used as a medicinal herb and an attractive landscape plant. Feverfew means "fever reducer," and it certainly lives up to the name. Traditionally, this plant, with its beautiful daisy-like flowers, was used to remedy fevers and inflammatory conditions. Some people even refer to it as "medieval aspirin."

Medicinal properties

Feverfew is known for its ability to remedy migraines, rheumatism, and arthritis, thanks to its anti-inflammatory, sedative, and antispasmodic properties. Chewing one to four leaves each day can help prevent migraines, and drinking the whole plant in a tea is a great way to relieve fever or cold symptoms. Many of the health benefits of feverfew stem from flavonoids, volatile oils, and parthenolide found in the leaves. Topical creams containing feverfew extract help ease irritated skin and acne by reducing inflammation. Feverfew may also help reduce symptoms of anxiety and depression.

Starting

Grow feverfew indoors or out. Indoors, it's best planted in small peat pots filled with damp soil. Sprinkle a few seeds and tap the bottom of the pot to help the seeds settle into the soil. Spray them lightly with water to keep them moist, and then place the pot in a sunny window. Outdoors, the process is much the same. Sow the seeds in early spring while the ground is still cool, sprinkling them and lightly tamping the soil without covering the seeds, as they require sunlight to germinate. Mist lightly with water to avoid washing the seeds away.

Growing tips

Apply a balanced light fertilizer in early spring and keep roots moist throughout the year - feverfew does not like dry conditions. Deadhead the spent blooms to prevent excessive re-seeding.

Harvesting

Harvest leaves at any time during the growing season and the flowers in early to mid-summer. Essential oil content peaks just as the plant begins to flower but before it is in full bloom. Harvest on a warm, dry day after the dew has dried off the plant. Use clean, sharp gardening shears or scissors to cut foliage and flowers cleanly. Leave the bottom two-thirds of the plant. Harvest again in three weeks.

Storing

Air dry by cutting stalks and placing them in bundles upside down in a dry, dark place for one week or more. You can also use a dehydrator at low heat to preserve essential oils. Once dried, remove leaves and flowers and store them in a glass jar with a tight-fitting lid in a dark pantry.

Try this

Add two tablespoons of dried leaves and blooms
to a cup of boiling water. Allow the mixture
to steep for five minutes, then strain and cool.
Apply to your skin before you go outdoors as a
natural insect repellent.

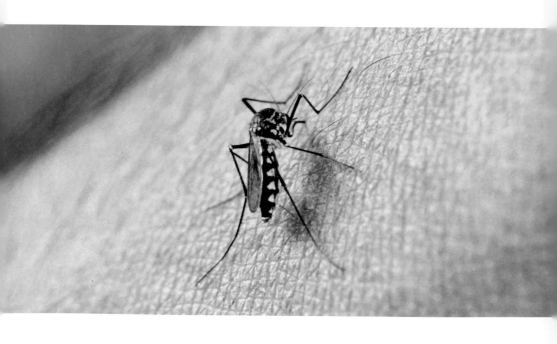

Garlic *(Allium sativum)*

Hardiness Zone: 1-7

Most people know garlic as a food and flavoring. Native to central Asia, many cultures use garlic for both culinary and medicinal purposes. This bulbous perennial is related to onions and has bulbs containing several cloves. Above ground, garlic leaves are long and grass-like. They develop an edible scape with a flower cluster on top that can be removed to stimulate bulb growth.

Medicinal properties

Although most people use garlic in the kitchen solely for its flavor, its use as a medicine and to promote good health in ancient times is well documented. Modern studies have found beneficial compounds in garlic, including sulfur compounds that give garlic its unique aroma. Garlic also boosts the immune system, reducing the number of colds and the length of illness while supporting heart health. Plus, it reduces blood pressure and lowers cholesterol levels. Antioxidants in garlic can reduce the risk of developing dementia and Alzheimer's disease.

Starting

Growing garlic is easy and inexpensive. Use cloves from a healthy bulb of garlic. Plant them outside in the fall. They'll begin to develop leaves in spring and are ready to harvest in summer. Timing is important. They need enough time to establish roots before the ground freezes but cannot be planted too soon as they'll grow leaves before winter. Plant them in a sunny spot where the soil is rich and slightly acidic, about two inches deep and two to four inches apart. Bury cloves with the paper on and the root side pointing down.

Growing tips

If you live in a cooler climate, cover planted cloves with mulch or straw for overwintering. Remove the cover after the risk of frost has passed in spring. Cut scapes off as they emerge so the plants can put energy into bulb formation. Garlic does not like competition, so keep the area weeded—water every few days from mid-May through June when the bulbs are developing.

Consider planting more than one variety of garlic for great flavor diversity. Also, if one variety has trouble taking off, you have others to depend on so that you always have plenty of garlic.

Harvesting

Garlic bulbs are ready to harvest from June to August, but this can change depending on the climate and planting time. Begin harvesting when the foliage yellows and falls over but before it is totally dry. Dig up the bulbs carefully and never pull them from the ground.

Storing

Garlic bulbs must be cured before storing and using them. Hang the bulbs upside down in a dry, shaded spot that gets good airflow. Once cured, store garlic in a cool, dry, dark spot for a few months. Do not keep it in the refrigerator.

Try this

Instead of buying garlic supplements, grow your own garlic and eat cloves raw for the medicinal benefits. An easy way to take raw garlic is to chop a couple of cloves into pill-sized pieces. Swallow them with water, as you would a pill. Alternatively, mince garlic and mix with a spoonful of honey to get it down more easily.

Ginger (*Zingiber officinale*)

Hardiness Zone: 8-12

Ginger is one of the most beloved herbs, with a wide range of uses in the kitchen and the medicine cabinet. It is excellent when made into a tea, pickled, used in stir-fries, and in a wide range of other recipes. Because ginger is a tropical plant, what you find in supermarkets usually comes from China, India, West Africa, and Indonesia. However, ginger will grow in warmer regions in America, such as Southern Arizona, Hawaii, Florida, southern Texas, Louisiana, and southern and coastal California. In cooler regions, ginger can be grown in containers.

Medicinal properties

This plant is an incredible source of antioxidants such as gingerols, zingerones, and shogaols. It also has anti-viral, antioxidant, and anti-parasitic properties, making it an excellent remedy to keep on hand at all times. Because it is an anti-inflammatory agent, ginger has been extensively studied for its pain-relieving properties. In one study, it was even shown to be more effective than ibuprofen in reducing menstrual symptoms in women. The pain relief isn't limited to muscle and joint ailments, either. If you suffer from migraines, ginger root could be a potent source of relief, and studies have compared its effectiveness to the migraine medication, Sumatriptan.

Most famous of all its benefits, however, is its ability to virtually eliminate nausea and digestive disturbances in even the most extreme circumstances. It has been proven effective for pregnant women suffering from morning sickness (be sure to consult your doctor before using this natural remedy during pregnancy). Plus, it can relieve nausea and vomiting following chemotherapy treatments in cancer patients, as well as motion sickness, and stomach upset from other causes.

Starting

Purchase a rhizome from a trusted supplier. You can get ginger from your grocery store, but be sure that it has plenty of eyes for growing. If you decide to start it outdoors, add plenty of compost or aged manure to the soil. Plant in early spring in an area that receives between two to five hours of direct sunlight and is protected from strong winds. Slice off fingers on the rhizome, making sure each piece is one to two inches long with at least one bud. Let the pieces dry for two days before planting. Place the cut sections eight inches apart and about three-quarters of an inch deep. Water deeply once a week. You should see leaves in about one week. Do not allow plants to dry out while they are growing. When the weather cools, reduce watering; this will encourage plants to form underground rhizomes. Ginger will grow up to four feet tall, and you may be able to see roots above the ground.

For container growing, plant indoors in the spring. Choose a healthy piece of ginger with plenty of eyes. Plant the ginger piece in a wide, shallow container at least 12 inches in diameter with good drainage and a rich potting mix. Plant the rhizome about three-quarters of an inch deep and water well. The soil should be wet down a few inches. Keep the pot in a warm area that receives indirect sunlight, and in just a week or so, you'll see new roots and shoots growing. Place some mulch on top of exposed roots to lock in moisture.

Growing tips

Ginger requires lots of moisture but also excellent drainage to prevent rot. The native climate for this plant is tropical, rainy, and forested, so if you are growing ginger in a dry climate, ensure that the soil does not dry out. Ginger plants do not like full sun but prefer some overhead shade.

Harvesting

The best time to harvest ginger from the garden is after 8 to 10 months. The most common way to harvest ginger is to dig it up. Rinse the dirt off under cold water and use the ginger as desired. Be sure to save some rhizomes for replanting. For container ginger, either wait to harvest it all or clip off small chunks of the rhizome as they appear above the soil line.

Storing

Fresh, unpeeled ginger keeps for about three weeks in the refrigerator and about six months in the freezer.

Try this

Make a dried ginger powder. Wash and dry a rhizome and slice into uniform slices. Place ginger pieces in a dehydrator until they are completely dry and snap under pressure. This will take about four hours. Place pieces in a spice grinder and process the ginger into a powder. Store in a spice jar

Globe Artichoke *(Cynara scolymus)*

Hardiness Zone: 7-11

Globe artichoke, not to be confused with Jerusalem artichoke, is usually enjoyed as a vegetable side; however, it has been used throughout history as a beneficial medicinal remedy in extracts and teas. Artichoke is native to North Africa and southern Europe and is related to daisies and thistles. Artichoke grows tall, up to six and a half feet, and produces a partially edible flower bud. The edible parts are the heart and the fleshy lower portions of the bracts, which are often called leaves. It is harvested to eat before the flower blooms.

Medicinal properties

Artichoke bracts (leaves) have several medicinal properties. Traditionally people used them to treat digestive and liver problems. Even when just viewed as a vegetable, artichoke is highly nutritious. It boasts significant amounts of fiber, protein, vitamins C and K, folic acid, magnesium, and several other nutrients. Modern research indicates that artichoke extract does have several medicinal properties, including lowering bad cholesterol and raising good cholesterol levels, regulating blood pressure, promoting liver health and bile production, and improving digestion by promoting healthy gut bacteria.

Starting

Artichoke grows well in warmer climates and is challenging to grow indoors simply because it is so large. If you have the right climate for it, start artichokes from seed directly outdoors in mid-spring. Sow two to three seeds together, a half-inch deep in decent soil.

Growing tips

In a suitable climate, artichoke isn't fussy. The soil should be at least a little fertile and drain well but shouldn't need much more than that. Once well-rooted, you don't need to water it often, only when conditions are dry. If grown as a perennial, each plant will need plenty of space to grow up to four feet tall and wide. Give it full sun or partial shade, and divide your plants every couple of years for five to six years of flowering. If winters bring frost, mulch over the area in late fall.

Harvesting

Artichoke buds are ready for harvest when they are compact and at least three inches across. The top bud will be ready first, usually in early summer. Don't wait until the buds begin to open, as they will not be as tender. Cut the stem a couple of inches below the bottom of the bud.

Storing

Artichoke buds are best eaten fresh. Store them in the refrigerator for up to two weeks.

Try this

For the health benefits, it's easy to cook and
enjoy this garden harvest. Steam the buds and
remove the bracts to eat the bottom, fleshy part,
and the heart deep inside the bud. Remove
the heart to use in all kinds of dishes, from
vegetable roasts to pizzas and salads.

Great Burdock *(Arctium lappa)*

Hardiness Zone: 2-10

Great burdock is also known as greater burdock, beggar's buttons, thorny burr, and other names. It's a weedy plant native to Europe and Asia that has become naturalized in much of North America. You'll find it in many disturbed areas along roadsides and in fields and parks - you'll likely recognize it by the burs it leaves on your pant legs. Great burdock is part of the aster family, with purple, heart-shaped leaves that look a little like thistles. The seeds, leaves, and roots are edible and have long been used in medicinal preparations.

Medicinal properties

Some of the historical medicinal uses for great burdock include the treatment of constipation, skin irritation, cold and flu, rheumatism, vertigo, burns, and many types of infections. It has also been used as a diuretic and a blood purifier. Studies have found that great burdock contains antioxidants and is anti-inflammatory and antimicrobial. Researchers have also found antidiabetic compounds in the plant and potential anticancer properties.

Starting

Great burdock is best started from seed. For better germination, soak the seeds in water overnight before planting. Prepare the soil down to at least 24 inches, as burdock grows deep roots. It should be rich and well-draining. Sow the seeds every six inches and a quarter-inch deep in early spring.

Growing tips

Once the seedlings grow larger, thin them so that they are 24 to 36 inches apart. Great burdock needs full sun or partial shade and plenty of water but not soggy soil. Provide regular vegetable fertilizer for the best results. Great burdock will do best in an outdoor bed, not in a container or indoors, due to the deep root and tall growth.

Harvesting

Pick off young leaves and stems to eat as you would other greens. The root is the most desirable part of the plant, however, both for food and medicine. To get a large root out of the ground, use a shovel and dig down deep as if you were digging out a tree. Young, small roots can be eaten raw, but mature roots must be cooked.

Plan accordingly when you plant burdock - it can grow up to ten feet tall in its second year of growth.

Storing

Use fresh leaves and roots of great burdock immediately in cooking. Store both in the vegetable drawer, but don't expect the leaves to last long. Dry the leaves to use in medicinal preparations, such as tea, and store them in airtight containers. The roots can be dried in small pieces using a food dehydrator or low oven temperature.

Try this

In cooking, use burdock root as you would
other root veggies like carrots or parsnips.
Roast the roots in the oven with oil and
salt for simple preparation. For a traditional
Japanese recipe, stir fry thin slices of burdock
root with carrot. Add soy sauce, mirin, sugar,
and saké to glaze the roots.

Great Mullein *(Verbascum thapsus)*

Hardiness Zone: 3-9

Great mullein is a biennial herb, or weed, depending on who you ask, that happily grows just about anywhere but will thrive in "difficult" spaces like between cracks in rocks, clay banks, or along a busy road. The amazing make-up of this plant allows it to use all available water expertly. Even the fuzzy leaves help with water retention, since the hairs provide shade to the leaves, lessening moisture loss via evaporation. All parts of the plant are useful and edible, and you don't have to worry about any poisonous compounds. Grand mullein is very tall in its second year, with soft leaves and yellow flowers at the top that give it a unique appearance.

Medicinal properties

Mullein contains powerful anti-viral and anti-inflammatory properties. Both the leaves and flowers help soothe respiratory conditions and can make coughs more productive. Traditional and contemporary anecdotal evidence suggests using great mullein for pain, constipation, inflammation, asthma, migraines, sleep, and gout. An infusion of the oils from the mullein flower can be used to make drops to ease earache. As a powerful antibacterial agent, it's very effective for treating mouth and gum ulcers and reducing the pain of a toothache.

Starting

Start seeds indoors six to eight weeks before the last frost in spring. Sprinkle seeds on the top of the potting soil before watering. It takes about two weeks for germination. Seeds can also be sown directly into the garden in late spring if you live in an area with a long growing season. Thin seedlings as they emerge and grow strong.

Growing tips

Mullein prefers full sun and a warm, dry location with lots of space to thrive. It grows in just about any type of soil, though it does best with dry, slightly alkaline soils. Keep the soil moist, especially when it flowers, but be careful not to overwater. Although fertilizer is not necessary, feeding with a slow-release balanced fertilizer at the beginning of the season fosters rapid growth and prolific blooms. This plant is frost resistant, but covering it with a layer of straw, leaves, or mulch before winter helps insulate the roots in cold regions.

Harvesting

Harvest flowers between June and October in the early morning. Leaves can be harvested in the first year, but second-year leaves will have more concentrated therapeutic compounds. If harvesting the root, simply pull the entire plant out of the ground. Don't forget to collect seeds from second-year plants.

You may know grand mullein by another of its many names, including duffle, fluffweed, goldenrod, Peter's staff, rag paper, velvet dock, wild ice leaf, woolly mullein, old man's flannel, or cowboy toilet paper.

Storing

Dry harvested mullein by hanging the entire plant in a dry place. Leaves can be placed on a drying rack or dehydrated. Wash roots carefully and allow them to dry on a rack or screen for a week. Store all parts in an airtight container for up to 18 months.

Try this

Add a handful of dried leaves to eight ounces of boiling water and steep for 20 minutes. Strain the leaves and add raw honey, cinnamon, and lemon. Sip slowly.

Jasmine (*Jasminum officinale*)

Hardiness Zone: 7-10

The name jasmine comes from the Persian word Yasmin, which means *"Gift from God."* The flower of this vining, shrub-like group of plants native to Asia is deemed sacred in India and the Himalayas and is the national flower of Pakistan and the Philippines. Common jasmine (Jasminum officinale) is a large, semi-evergreen, or deciduous climbing shrub that grows rapidly and produces large, beautiful, and very fragrant flowers that bloom from late spring through fall. But beauty and fragrance are not all this *"Queen of Flowers,"* has to offer - it is also highly respected for its health benefits. If you want an evening-blooming interest spot in your garden, plant jasmine - its beautiful flowers open up towards the end of the day and into the evening.

Medicinal properties

Most of the benefits of jasmine are found when it is made into a tea using green tea leaves or as an essential oil. Jasmine is loaded with antioxidants and can promote healthy heart function and reduce the risk of heart conditions. It contains

Beware: Common jasmine is a relative of frangipani and star jasmine, which are toxic plants with poisonous sap.

anticoagulant and anti-fibrinolytic properties that help reduce "bad" cholesterol, prevent blockage, and lower the risk of clots in the arteries leading to abnormal heart rhythms, heart attack, or conditions such as atherosclerosis. Jasmine also contains EGCG (epigallocatechin and gallic acid) in the leaves, which can help speed up metabolism and prevent weight gain.

Jasmine contains salicylic acid, the active component in aspirin, and it could be useful as an anti-inflammatory agent to relieve pain. Hypoglycemic properties of jasmine flowers help lower blood sugar, while regular consumption of jasmine tea or foods prepared with jasmine help reduce the breakdown of starch into glucose which lowers fasting blood sugar and insulin levels.

Antioxidants and polyphenols found in the flower help the body make mood-enhancing neurotransmitters, including serotonin and dopamine. Additionally, it promotes memory capacity, focus, concentration, alertness, and calmness. Because of this, jasmine is often considered a remedy for depression and insomnia, and it can be helpful for ailments like Alzheimer's and Parkinson's disease.

Antioxidants in jasmine also mingle with gastric enzymes to improve digestion, relieve abdominal pain, and help ease symptoms of irritable bowel syndrome. It has even been found that jasmine can help promote healthy bacteria in the gut while reducing bad bacteria. Catechins found in jasmine tea fight bacteria that cause bad breath and plaque, reducing the risk of cavities.

Starting

Start jasmine seeds - after soaking for 24 hours- about three months before you estimate that your temperatures will consistently reach 70 degrees or more. Plant one seed per starter pot or cell, water well, and cover loosely with a clear plastic bag to create a greenhouse effect. Repot seedlings when they have two pairs of true leaves and keep your plant indoors for at least a month after this - or grow as a houseplant.

You can also start jasmine from a cutting taken from an established and healthy jasmine plant. Use stem tips, cutting a five-inch piece just below a leaf. Strip leaves from the lower portion of the cutting and dip the stem in rooting hormone. Place the cutting in a container filled with damp sand and cover it loosely with a clear plastic bag. Keep the bag somewhere that is 75 degrees F or warmer and out of direct sunlight. Ensure that the sand is always moist, and you will see roots begin to develop in a month. After this, you can transplant to a container with potting soil for at least a month before transplanting outdoors.

Growing tips

Provide a sturdy trellis and train vines early. Give your jasmine plant a balanced organic fertilizer in the spring before new growth appears. To encourage a bushy growing habit, pinch the tips of the vine in the second year. Dwarf varieties are quite happy being grown as container plants indoors. Provide even moisture, plenty of sunlight, fertilize twice a year, and you will get to enjoy this lovely plant in your home all year long.

Harvesting

The best time to harvest jasmine flowers is in the early morning when the flowers are closed. Pull off individual flowers or snip branches for a bigger harvest.

Storing

Use fresh jasmine immediately or hang bundles in a cool, dry, and dark place. Once dry, pull flowers off of the branches and store them in an airtight container.

Try this

Make your very own jasmine massage oil by adding one cup of blossoms to one cup of jojoba oil in a glass jar with an airtight lid. Place the jar in the windowsill and allow the blooms to infuse into the oil for two weeks. Shake the jar daily. Use a coffee filter to strain out blossoms and enjoy.

Jiaogulan *(Gynostemma pentaphyllum)*

Hardiness Zone: 8-10

Jiaogulan, also known as southern ginseng, fairy herb, and sweet tea vine, is a plant that grows wild in Asia, primarily in south-central China. It is in the same family as melons, gourds, and cucumbers and was originally combined with black tea leaves to sweeten them. This short-lived perennial is often referred to as the immortality herb and is believed to promote a long, healthy life free from disease. Jiaogulan can grow to over 20-feet long, which means it has the potential to be an invasive species and requires regular upkeep to keep under control. Inconspicuous flowers appear on this vine in mid-to-late summer and turn into round, green seed pods if male and female plants are near each other. The leaves are most often used for medicinal purposes; however, the entire plant is edible.

Medicinal properties

Southern ginseng can calm or energize the system, depending on the body's particular needs. It contains saponins that can positively affect blood pressure, cholesterol levels, the immune system, blood sugar levels, endurance, and more. Its gypenosides have also been used in cancer and hepatitis treatment. This plant can even be used as cough remedy, to treat chronic bronchitis, to reduce pain and swelling, and to limit insomnia.

Starting

Soak seeds in warm water for 24 hours before planting. Start in a moist potting mix indoors 8 to 10 weeks before your last known spring frost or sow directly into the garden once the soil has warmed. Because they often have poor germination rates, use a larger pot and plant three seeds in each in a triangular pattern when starting indoors. Place the pot in an east or west-facing window where plants will receive partial sun or keep under grow lights for 12 hours a day. Water regularly to keep the soil moist. You can also propagate by placing a cutting from a mature vine in a glass of water until roots form. Transplant into a container or into the garden.

Jiaogulan is referred to as the new ginseng because it offers many of the same chemical compounds found in ginseng.

Growing

Jiaogulan prefers to be sheltered in partial shade or grown indoors on a bright window sill that faces east or west. Whether you choose to grow it indoors or out, use rich, well-drained soil and keep it moist but not waterlogged. Provide a sturdy trellis for this plant so that it has something for its curly tendrils to hang onto. Place plants one foot from the lattice and provide a two inch layer of mulch. Once the vine takes off, it will grow quickly and require little care other than the occasional drink of water. Because plants are either male or female, plant one of each nearby if you wish to harvest seeds.

Harvesting

Harvest once the plant has reached one and a half feet tall. Cut vines into three to five inch pieces and dry the leaves on the stem by placing them on a screen in a cool, dark, dry location. You can also use a food dehydrator and dehydrate until crisp.

Storing

Hang stems and leaves to dry in a well-ventilated, dry room away from sunlight. Store dried leaves and stems in an airtight container.

Try this

Prepare fairy herb tea by heating filtered water and adding two teaspoons of dried leaf. Steep for 10 minutes and add some raw honey for sweetener. **Note:** leaves can be left steeping for up to two hours to extract beneficial properties and increase flavor.

Johnny-Jump-Up *(Viola tricolor)*

Hardiness Zone: 3-8

Also known as heart's ease, tickle-my-fancy, and field pansy, johnny jump-ups are part of the pansy family and have dainty flowers that look like miniature pansies. They are annual, bi-annual, or short-lived perennial, depending on your growing zone, and come in many colors, including deep violet, yellow, mauve, and white. The blossoms not only add color to this adorable plant, but they're edible as well, with a mild wintergreen flavor. They're often used in desserts, soups, salads, and drinks for a tasty, visually appealing garnish. Grow johnny jump ups in pots in an indoor herb garden or on a porch or patio to enjoy a plant that is a delight for the eyes, a tasty treat, and a medicinal powerhouse.

Medicinal properties

Johnny Jump Ups are rich in antifungal and anti-inflammatory properties. They have traditionally been incorporated into herbal remedies to treat wounds and sores externally, but infusions of the plant can be used for many things, including sore throats, coughs, high blood pressure, and intestinal issues. Known as a natural aspirin, these pretty plants are also good for minor aches and pains.

Starting

Start seeds indoors six to eight weeks before the last known spring frost date. Sow seeds one inch apart in a lightweight seedling mix and barely cover them with potting mix. Keep them moist and warm and provide a light source until they are ready to transplant in the spring. Transplant four to five inches apart in the garden or pot once they are large enough to handle. They take a bit to germinate, so be patient. You can also directly sow them outdoors in the spring in an area with full or partial sun. To save time, buy plants from your local nursery that are established and ready to go.

Growing tips

Johnny jump ups prefer rich soil that drains well. Although this little plant loves sunshine, it is not as fond of heat, making it a perfect early spring or fall option. Jump ups readily self-seed, which is a nice bonus, and in warmer areas, they behave as a perennial. These miniature pansy look-alikes bloom from early spring through fall as long as you frequently deadhead them.

Harvesting

To harvest edible flowers when they are at the peak of freshness, wait until they are in full bloom and not wilting. Harvest only in the early morning or late evening when it is cool. This will ensure that cut flowers will have plenty of water content and be fresh and perky. Harvest one-third of the blooms to encourage more flowers.

Storing

Use edible flowers within a day - it's best if you use them right away. When harvesting, use a clean pair of micro-tip pruning shears and cut the bloom just below the flower head. Edible flowers are fragile and will last for a few days in a basket in the fridge. They may keep for up to six days if you place them in an airtight container.

If flowers turn droopy, place them in an ice bath for 10 minutes to revive. Be sure to use them immediately after taking them out of the ice bath.

Try this

To help ease coughing, make a johnny jump up tea. Place flower petals inside a teapot and pour boiling water over the top of them. Allow them to steep for five minutes, then strain. Add some raw honey and a slice of lemon.

Lamb's Ear *(Stachys byzantina)*

Hardiness Zone: 4-7

Kids, adults, and pollinators love this plant with its soft, fuzzy leaves. Lamb's ear is a popular, easy-care perennial native to Turkey, Armenia, and Iran, with pretty, silver-gray evergreen leaves similar in shape to a real lamb's ear - hence its name. If left to bloom, lamb's ear will shoot up spikes of pink to purplish colored flowers in summer. This plant, known as the "band-aid" plant, is used for medicinal purposes such as wound healing and bee sting relief.

Medicinal properties

For centuries, this woolly plant, sometimes known as woolly betony, was used for hemorrhoids, menstrual flow, and even delivering babies. With the invention of gauze and feminine hygiene products, the use of lamb's ear for these purposes disappeared. However, its leaves have powerful analgesic, anti-inflammatory, antispasmodic, astringent, and antibacterial properties and are often employed as a dressing or poultice. Lambs ears are also delicious in salads or steamed gently as greens. The taste is fruity - like a delightful combination of apples and pineapples. Teas prepared with lambs ear help with sore throats, staph infections, gout, hypertension, asthma, kidney stones, and headaches.

Urban legend has it that this woolly plant was the first toilet tissue. If you are ever out on a camping or hiking trip and need to go - look for lamb's ear!

Starting

Start seeds indoors eight to ten weeks before the last predicted spring frost. Seeds can also be started outdoors in the spring and the fall. Gently press seeds into the soil and lightly cover for best results. Germination takes about 30 days on average. Transplant or thin plants to one plant every foot to give them room to spread out. Lamb's ear will happily self-seed if you leave spent flowers on the stalk. Transplant seedlings once they have three sets of true leaves.

Growing tips

Lamb's ear plants are low maintenance and, once established, drought-tolerant. They do well in full sun or partial shade and tolerate extremely poor soil. They also do well in container gardens. Water when soil is significantly dry and use mulch under leaves to keep them from rotting in humid conditions. Trim in the spring and cut out dead and brown leaves. If you don't want the plant to spread, be sure to deadhead spent blooms and divide regularly. Once established, plants are easy to propagate and move to different areas or just give some away! Do this in the spring or fall.

Harvesting

Snip leaves just before the plant flowers using shears. Use the leaves fresh, steamed, or dried. To dry, spread the leaves out on a newspaper in a dry location. Because they're so thick, it takes between two to four weeks for the leaves to dry. You can also use a dehydrator to dry leaves if you want to speed up the process.

Storing

Store dried leaves in a clean jar with a lid. Store fresh leaves for a few days in the refrigerator, pressed between two damp paper towels.

Try this

Pack a few fresh leaves with you when you go camping or hiking. Leaves are perfect for easing the sting of insect bites and helping speed up the healing of minor cuts. Plus, you can always use it as toilet paper and don't have to worry about littering. It's all natural!

Lavender *(Lavandula angustifolia)*

Hardiness Zone: 5-8

Lavender, a member of the mint family, is one of the most popular herbs used in the natural health and beauty industry. Few scents evoke the feeling of cleanliness and calm that this tender perennial does. There are 39 species of lavender, most native to Eastern Europe, northern Africa, western Asia, and the Mediterranean. English lavender (*Lavandula angustifolia)* is the most common species grown and used medicinally.

This herb is a delight, with its sweet, floral flavor and lemon and citrus notes. It grows about two to three feet tall and has gray-green leaves and pretty purplish flowers that appear in late spring. In warmer climates, the leaves may be green all year long. The flowers add beautiful color to salads, and they can also make a great alternative to rosemary in bread and baking recipes. Lavender oil smells fantastic, tastes amazing, and has many potential health benefits that you may not even know about. This calming herb can bring you peace and relaxation on even the most stressful day.

Medicinal properties

Lavender has anti-inflammatory, antifungal, antidepressant, antiseptic, antibacterial, and antimicrobial properties. Plus, it has been shown to help alleviate anxiety, depression, and insomnia in many instances due to its sedative nature. Because lavender is slightly bitter, many herbalists use it as a bile stimulant and liver tonic. As a gentle digestive aid, it is often used to treat intestinal gas, nausea, and irritable bowel syndrome.

Because of its antifungal and antibacterial properties, lavender oil is a powerful tool for eliminating skin ailments such as acne, eczema, and psoriasis and could even speed up the healing process for wounds and burns. Lavender oil works to open the lungs as well, which means that it may be beneficial in relieving upper respiratory problems like coughing, asthma, sinus congestion, bronchitis, and laryngitis. When applied to the neck, chest, or back in a balm form or inhaled through various aromatherapy methods, it can soothe irritated lungs and act as a sleep aid. Lavender oil can be applied topically when mixed with a carrier oil or used in an air diffuser or vaporizer.

Starting

Although it isn't as easy to start lavender seeds as other seeds, it can be done. However, the easiest way to start lavender plants is from cuttings or small plants purchased at your local plant nursery.

Growing tips

You can grow lavender indoors or out, though the plants do best outdoors. The English type is not only the sweetest and most widely grown, but it has a good tolerance for winter moisture and humidity as well. Make sure plants get at least six hours of full sun each day. Water young plants well but very little once they are mature. Lavender plants prefer slightly sandy, neutral pH, well-draining soil. Once established, it is best to prune new spring growth by cutting about one-third of the green stalks. Cut the entire plant down to eight inches from the ground in early spring once every three years to promote new growth and control the plant's size. Provide a layer of mulch for winter protection in cooler regions.

Harvesting

Harvest lavender when the buds have formed, but the flowers are not yet open. Closed buds retain fragrance and color longer. Use clean, sharp bypass pruners and gather a small handful of long flower stems. When you harvest, leave behind at least two sets of leaves on the green part of the stem - do not cut back to the woody part.

Storing

Hang bunches of lavender, tied with twine, in a warm and dry spot away from direct sunlight. A well-ventilated garage works well, as does a shady fence. After about three weeks, lavender should be thoroughly dried. Gently rub the buds into a bowl and store them in a jar with a tight lid in a cool, dark place.

Try this

Make a de-stressing sachet by filling an empty sachet with dried lavender. Sew the end shut and gently squeeze the bag to release the calming aroma.

Lemon Balm *(Melissa officinalis)*

Hardiness Zone: 4-9

A member of the mint family, lemon balm is most noted for its sweet, soothing lemony scent. Small, white flowers bloom in tight clusters at the axles along the length of the stem throughout the summer and into fall. The medicinal properties of this perennial herb date back to the ancient Greeks and Romans, who often referred to it as a "cure-all," employing lemon balm as a treatment for everything from stomach upset to topical cures for skin ailments. Even earlier writings suggest that this aromatic herb was a staple among healers as far back as 300 B.C.

Medicinal properties

Thanks to lemon balm's high concentration of phytochemicals, the herb can be used to remedy several ailments. While historically used as a treatment for practically everything, recent research has noted that the herb's mood-elevating and anti-anxiety properties may be helpful in treating depression and related conditions. Other research has focused on lemon balm's antiviral properties, noting that it can fight sores caused by the Herpes virus and reduce the infectivity of HIV in exposed patients.

Starting

Lemon balm does best when grown from small plants. Transplant into the garden after all danger of frost has passed. One plant per square foot.

Lemon balm is a great plant to grow with children as most love the fuzzy leaves and lemon scent.

Growing tips

Lemon balm will grow indoors as long as it gets as much direct light as possible, at least six hours of solid sunlight each day. It also likes a steady supply of water, but it needs good drainage. Outdoors, it can be grown in just about any climate in an area that gets lots of sun - though some shade during the day is okay. Use rich, moist, well-draining soil and a little organic fertilizer too. Lemon balm does not spread by underground runners like mint, but it will still spread seeds and begin to take over the garden if left unchecked. Trim it back to several inches tall a few times during the growing season.

Harvesting

Harvest fresh leaves any time once plants are mature. If you plan on drying the leaves, it is best to wait to harvest until you see flower buds. This is the time when the oils in the leaves are most potent. Using clean, sharp pruning shears, cut each stem directly above a pair of leaves. Although a second harvest may be possible in the fall, the first harvest is always the sweetest and most aromatic.

Storing

Wash and dry fresh lemon balm leaves and store them in a plastic bag in the refrigerator for up to five days. Another fun way to preserve lemon balm is to wash and dry leaves and place them in a sterilized glass jar. Fill the jar with olive oil and store it in the refrigerator for two months. Whole leaves also keep for up to six months in an airtight container in the freezer.

Try this

Make a delicious marinade or salad dressing using fresh lemon balm. Combine two cups of fresh leaves with one tablespoon of minced garlic, a quarter teaspoon garlic powder, one tablespoon molasses, and half a cup of virgin olive oil.

Lemongrass *(Cymbopogon citratus)*

Hardiness Zone: 9-10

Most people associate lemongrass with southeast Asian cuisine. Native to tropical Asia and parts of India, lemongrass is a tasty herb for cooking and a valuable medicinal plant. The name describes the aroma and flavor, lemon-like and perfect in many savory and sweet dishes and drinks.

Lemongrass grows like ornamental grass, which means that many gardeners use it decoratively and for practical harvest. It grows quickly, up to four feet tall, and turns pretty shades of red in fall.

Medicinal properties

The most common medicinal preparations use lemongrass as an essential oil and a tea. In some Asian cultures, lemongrass is also called fever grass. People have long used the tea to treat fevers, and modern studies have confirmed many of the medicinal properties of this plant. It contains antioxidants and is antimicrobial and anti-inflammatory. Because of this, it may be useful for reducing blood pressure, decreasing cancer risk, lowering cholesterol, and as a diuretic and digestion aid.

Starting

Lemongrass is easy to start from seed directly outdoors. In tropical areas, sow seeds evenly in spring, barely covering with soil. If your soil is poor, prepare it first by adding organic material or fertilizer. Lemongrass prefers rich soil. If you live in a colder climate, start seeds indoors in containers. You can easily grow this plant inside or move the container outdoors for summer, bringing it in for the winter.

Growing tips

Provide lemongrass with full sun and plenty of heat and humidity to mimic a tropical environment. The soil should stay evenly moist. A layer of mulch helps keep water in the ground. Water lemongrass regularly as it establishes its roots. For fertilizer, choose a nitrogen-rich product to encourage growth. A slow-release 6-4-0 fertilizer is a good option.

Harvesting

Harvest parts of your lemongrass plant as needed. Even when young, it will tolerate occasional harvests because it grows so fast. Remove leaves to steep for tea and the flesh stalks for cooking. The leaves are too tough to eat. To harvest stalks, use a trowel to remove the roots and stalk together.

While lemongrass is edible and safe for humans, it can cause an upset stomach in cats and dogs. If growing pots of lemongrass indoors, keep out of reach of pets. Outside, keep it in beds that animals with outdoor access cannot reach.

Storing

Dry leaves to store for tea and medicinal preparations. Use the stalks fresh or store them by removing the outer leaves first and freeze the stalk whole or chop it into small pieces.

Try this

A tea is the simplest way to get the benefits of lemongrass for medicinal purposes. Use about one teaspoon of dried leaves in a cup of boiling water. Steep for several minutes and strain out the leaves. Try adding a few lemongrass leaves to other teas to add flavor. Lemongrass goes very well with green tea and other herbal blends.

Marsh Mallow *(Althaea officinalis)*

Hardiness Zone: 3-9

Marsh Mallow is a perennial native to North Africa, Europe, and western Asia. It is the origin of the confection we call marshmallow today. Since ancient times, people used the root of this plant medicinally and in food that evolved into modern marshmallows. Marsh mallow has naturalized in much of the U.S. You'll find it growing on the edges of marshy areas, on grassy banks near ditches, and in other wet areas. Marsh mallow grows up to four feet tall and has hairy leaves and stems, while the flowers have five petals tinged with pink.

Medicinal properties

The flowers, roots, and leaves of marsh mallow are all edible and have long been used in food. The roots, when boiled, create a gelatinous substance, the origin of marshmallows. People have also utilized the plant as a medicine since ancient times, and its use has been recorded in Egypt, Rome, and Syria.

The entire plant has medicinal properties, but they are most concentrated in the root. Use marsh mallow root to treat coughs and other cold symptoms, to relieve skin inflammation and irritation, to promote wound healing, as a diuretic, and to aid digestion and soothe irritation in the gut.

Starting

Stratification is important if starting from seed. Place seeds in the refrigerator for a few weeks before sowing to simulate the dormant period necessary for germination. Sow seeds indoors four weeks before the last frost or directly outside after the danger has passed. You can easily grow marsh mallow in containers indoors or out.

Growing tips

Space marsh mallow plants 18 to 24 inches apart in beds or pots in soil that retains moisture well. It prefers damp soil, so a spot near a river or wetlands is ideal. If growing in containers, you will need to water the plants daily. Water regularly outdoors in beds if the plants are not placed in a marshy area. Full sun is best, but marsh mallow will tolerate morning sun and afternoon shade.

Harvesting

Harvest the leaves of marsh mallow at any time. The roots are best harvested in the fall. Wait until the second year of growth to ensure the roots are large enough to be worth pulling from the ground. It is possible, with care, to remove some of the roots and put the crown back in the soil for next year's growth.

Storing

Mars hmallow roots are most often used dried. After harvesting the roots, clean them thoroughly, chop them into small pieces, and dry. Use a dehydrator or the oven on a low setting to dry them until they are hard and brittle. You can then store them indefinitely in an airtight container.

Try this

Make marsh mallow tea to soothe a cough or an upset stomach. Steep a tablespoon of dried marsh mallow roots in a cup of warm, not boiling water. Let it steep for several hours, up to eight. Strain the roots before drinking. For a better flavor, add peppermint or lemon verbena to the steeping water.

Meadowsweet *(Filipendula ulmaria)*

Hardiness Zone: 3-8

Meadowsweet is a perennial native to Europe and Asia that is well naturalized in North America. In many areas, it is considered an invasive weed. Also known as mead wort and queen of the meadow, meadowsweet grows in upright clumps to about three or four feet tall. It produces four to six-inch panicles of creamy white flowers and compound leaves with hairy, whitish undersides. Meadowsweet has long been used as medicine and to flavor drinks and make tea. It was also strewn on floors as a rudimentary air freshener because of its characteristic sweet aroma.

Medicinal properties

Traditionally, people used meadowsweet to treat joint pain, heartburn, stomach pain and ulcers, gout, colds, and kidney infections. Modern research into meadowsweet's medicinal properties is limited. Some studies show the potential for it to be anti-inflammatory and antibacterial, and animal studies have shown some anti-tumor properties as well. Meadowsweet contains tannins and flavonoids, which are antioxidants.

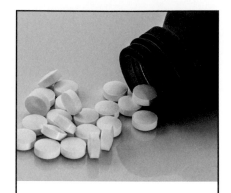

Thank meadowsweet for aspirin. A Bayer chemist synthesized a compound that became aspirin from the meadowsweet plant. This is likely why people have long used it for joint pain and arthritis.

Starting

It's best to start meadowsweet indoors. The seeds need light to germinate, so they shouldn't be pushed into the soil. If left outside on the surface of the soil, they may blow away or be eaten. Scatter seeds on the surface of the soil in starting trays and keep by a sunny window. Be patient, as they can take up to three weeks to germinate.

Growing tips

Transplant meadowsweet outdoors when the danger of frost has passed. It prefers wet soil, so plant near streams or ponds or in a low area that collects rain. Meadowsweet likes full sun but can tolerate some shade. Fertilizer isn't necessary, but don't expect significant growth in the first year. The plants will grow to full size in year two.

Harvesting

Both the leaves and flowers of meadowsweet are edible and have similar properties, but the flowers are more often used in culinary preparations. Harvest the leaves at any time. But for the best flavor, wait until just before the flowers bloom. Pick the panicles of flowers early in the day with shears or scissors.

Storing

You can use the flowers fresh or dried. Dry the leaves on a screen and keep them in an airtight container for later use in tea or other medicinal preparations. Use the leaves fresh as greens, either raw or cooked. Dry the flowers by hanging them upside down. Store in a paper bag if you intend to use them within a few weeks.

Try this

Use meadowsweet in a steam bath to treat inflammatory skin conditions like acne. Use two teaspoons of dried leaves or flowers, or a larger amount of fresh flowers, and enough water to fill a large bowl. Bring the water to a boil and let it cool for a minute before adding to the meadowsweet. Bring your face over the bowl and tent a towel over your head to trap in the steam. Breathe deeply and remain under the towel for about five minutes. This will open up your pores and help clear up acne and other inflammatory skin conditions.

Motherwort *(Leonurus cardiaca)*

Hardiness Zone: 4-8

This spiky and clumping perennial plant blossoms in late summer, with its tall stalks, flowers, and leaves often harvested for use in herbal medicine. It is often found growing in wet areas such as floodplains and along streams and riverbanks, and it pops up as a common weed along roadsides and in neglected gardens. A member of the mint family, this herb is a prolific, sometimes invasive grower. Clusters of pink to purple flowers appear on prickly sepals and bloom from mid-summer through early fall. The tooth-like leaf structure is quite unique and a great help in identifying this medicinal plant.

Medicinal properties

The botanical name leonurus cardiaca means "lion-hearted" and is related to the plant's reputation for bringing strength and relief during times of emotional stress and reducing anxiety and irritability. It also provides support to the circulatory system.

In Nicolas Culpeper's 1653 book, *"The Complete Herbal,"* he says this about motherwort, "it makes women joyful mothers of children, and seetles their wombs as they should be, therefore we call it Motherwort." Additionally, the medieval botanist, herbalist, and physician claims that it is of great use for the heart and states that this is where the name cardiaca comes from. Motherwort is useful as an aid for symptoms of menopause, including mood swings, insomnia, and hot flashes. In Germany, this plant has been approved for use in nervous conditions and to treat hypothyroidism.

Starting

Before starting seeds, they must be cold stratified. To do this, soak seeds for 12-24 hours and then put them in a plastic bag filled with a 50/50 mixture of sand and peat. Place the sealed bag in the refrigerator for 10 days. Check seeds regularly and spritz with water if they become dry. Sow seeds directly into the garden in late spring by broadcasting. Cover with one-eighth of an inch of soil. It takes a week or so for seeds to sprout. Thin plants so that there is two feet between them.

Growing

While it's very forgiving, motherwort is best grown outdoors and sown directly into your garden. It grows well in all light conditions and in most soils. Keep young plants watered daily until they are established. As it self-seeds like crazy, it's important not to let it reseed unless you want it to take over an entire area. You can limit the chances of this occurring by cutting it back to three to five inches after flowering before the seeds mature.

One of the best ways to acquire motherwort is to find a patch already growing and cut some divisions. Take a Sunday drive and be on the lookout for this unique plant.

Harvesting

The best time to harvest motherwort is in the early to mid-summer, right before it flowers. You can also harvest the big and soft leaves after flowering. Put on some gloves to protect your hands, and then use clean shears to snip off the top third of stems, including the leaves, flowers, and buds.

Storing

To dry motherwort, make bundles using garden twine and hang them in an airy, dry location. Alternatively, you can also use a screen for drying. To speed up drying, use a dehydrator on low heat. Remove leaves and flowers from stems and store them in a clean glass jar with a lid in a dark pantry or cupboard.

Try this

Make an herbal vinegar by filling a jar halfway with dried motherwort. Cover with apple cider vinegar. Place a nonreactive plastic lid on the jar and let it sit in a pantry for a month - shaking daily. Strain out solids and keep the vinegar in a cool, dark location. It will stay fresh for two years.

Nasturtium *(Tropaeolum spp.)*

Hardiness Zone: 2-11

Nasturtium refers to a species of flowering herbs native to Central and South America grown as annuals in nearly all climates. It is sometimes called Indian cress, referring to its origins in the West Indies. The flowers come in cheerful red, orange, and yellow hues and bloom from May through September.

Medicinal properties

The flowers and leaves of nasturtium are edible and are often used raw in salads. They are highly nutritious as well, containing potassium, calcium, magnesium, copper, zinc, iron, and other nutrients. Nasturtium also contains compounds that provide medicinal benefits. They are antimicrobial and antifungal, act as an expectorant, and may even have anti-cancer properties. Studies have also shown that the flowers contain antioxidants and have anti-inflammatory effects. Nasturtium has even been used to treat kidney disease and urinary tract infections, but modern evidence does not necessarily support these uses.

Starting

Nasturtium is easy to grow from seed. Start seeds indoors two to four weeks before the last frost or outside two weeks after the last frost. It doesn't require rich soil and actually thrives in poor soil, but it should be well-draining. Plant the seeds 10 to 12 inches apart and about a half-inch deep in the soil.

Growing tips

Provide nasturtium with full sun or partial shade. Give trailing types something to climb, such as a fence or trellis. Water regularly but take care not to overwater or create soggy soil. Nasturtium will tolerate some drought but keep in mind; the plants will produce less in extreme summer heat. Provide some shade and more water under these conditions. Deadhead the flowers to keep blooms coming through the growing season. Nasturtium thrives in many conditions with minimal upkeep and doesn't require any fertilizer.

Harvesting

Harvest flowers and leaves to use fresh whenever you need them. You can also eat the seed pods as long as you harvest them before they have hardened. Use scissors or shears to collect seed pods to avoid plant damage.

Storing

Use fresh leaves and flowers as soon after harvesting as possible. Keep them in the vegetable drawer of the refrigerator for just a couple of days. You can eat the seeds raw too, but they also stand up to pickling for longer storage.

Try this

To get the health benefits of nasturtium, make pickled seeds. Mix a cup of white vinegar, a teaspoon of salt, and six peppercorns and bring to a boil. Pour the mixture over a cup of fresh, green nasturtium seeds in a canning jar. Let them pickle in the refrigerator for about three months. Eat the leaves and flowers of nasturtium if you feel a cold coming on or have a respiratory infection. It is no substitute for medical care but may shorten the duration of an infection.

Oregano *(Origanum vulgare)*

Hardiness Zone: 5-10

Oregano is a popular herb used in Italian cuisine and on pizza, but it has a long, rich history of medicinal use. It is an herbaceous perennial native to Europe and Asia that grows like a bush with woody stems. The leaves and flowers of oregano are similar to mint, as it is in the same family, but the leaves are smaller and round, while the flowers are small and white or pink-purple. Use the fragrant leaves in cooking and medicinal preparations.

Medicinal properties

Medicinal use of oregano dates back thousands of years. Native to the Mediterranean, it was a popular herb for healers in ancient Greece and Rome. Today, researchers have proven many of the benefits and medicinal uses of oregano. It is rich in antioxidants and has antibacterial and anti-inflammatory properties and may also be effective in combating viral infections. Some research using cancer cells indicates that oregano has anti-cancer properties as well, but more testing is needed to confirm. The most proven, effective use of oregano is for treating bacterial infections, with proven action against at least 23 different types of bacteria.

The Romans and Greeks associated oregano with happiness and joy. The name is derived from the Greeks words "oros," meaning mountain, and "ganos," meaning joy.

Starting

Grow oregano from seed or cuttings. Sow seeds or put out cuttings after the last frost of spring. Oregano also grows easily in containers outside or indoors by a sunny window. As seedlings grow, thin them to provide 8 to 10 inches between plants.

Growing tips

Oregano needs full sun and soil that ranges from dry to medium moisture. It should drain well, but it generally needs less water than other herbs; only water plants when the soil feels dry at least an inch down. As the oregano grows, pinch off the tips of stems to encourage a bushier habit. Oregano will self-seed, so let the flowers stay in place to get more plants in subsequent years.

Harvesting

You'll get the best flavor harvesting leaves just before the plant flowers if you are using them for culinary purposes. For medicinal use, harvest leaves at any time. Pull off leaves as you need them or cut whole stems to get a larger harvest.

Storing

Use fresh leaves immediately or dry them to preserve them for longer. Spread them out on a screen or drying tray in a dry, sheltered area. Let them dry out completely and then crumble the leaves before storing them in an airtight container. You can also keep oregano leaves in the freezer for future culinary use.

Try this

Make oregano tea for an antioxidant boost or to soothe a sore throat. It may help relieve digestive problems as well and acts as a diuretic to reduce bloat. Steep two teaspoons of dried oregano leaves in a cup of boiling water for two to four minutes. Strain before drinking.

Parsley *(Petroselinum crispum)*

Hardiness Zone: 5-9

Parsley is one of the most well-known herbs. It is easy to incorporate into many dishes and adds flavor and nutrients to salads, pasta dishes, soups, stews, stir-fries, and much more. It is easy to tell that this Mediterranean native plant is a member of the carrot family by its feathery leaves. Flat-leaf varieties are often used in cooking, and curly-leaf varieties make a beautiful garnish.

Medicinal properties

Antioxidants, including vitamin C, A, and E in parsley help reduce inflammation. This herb is also a rich source of flavonoids, antioxidants credited with reducing the risk of a host of chronic diseases, including atherosclerosis, Parkinson's disease, and Alzhemiers's. Parsley also contains vitamin K (10 sprigs provides your daily dose), necessary for blood clotting and bone health.

Eating parsley is good for your skin as well since the vitamin C in parsley makes collagen, which gives skin its structure and strength. Additionally, parsley is a soothing herb that can calm an angry digestive system and reduce bloating. Homeopathic practitioners use parsley to ease urinary tract infections and kidney and bladder stones. Raw parsley also contains important B vitamins that are good for the heart and include a hefty iron dose. Don't forget to munch on some parsley to keep your breath smelling fresh.

The word parsley comes from the Greek word Petros meaning "stone," as this dainty plant was often found growing between rocks.

Starting

Soak the seeds in warm water first to crack the seed coat. To get a jump on the season, start parsley seeds indoors in individual pots about eight weeks before the last known spring frost date. Sprinkle seeds onto the surface of the soil and then cover them up with another quarter-inch of soil. Water regularly, keeping the soil moist to the touch but never soggy. For direct sowing into the garden, plant seeds about a quarter-inch deep in rich, well-draining soil. Leave about six inches between seeds.

Growing tips

Parsley does best in a sunny, south-facing window or two inches below a grow light indoors, and in a full-sun location outdoors. Keep parsley plants well-watered and provide a light layer of mulch to help retain moisture.

Harvesting

Parsley is generally ready for harvest between 70-90 days after planting. Cut sprigs from the outside down to the soil level or bunch a group of leaves and snip them off at soil level.

Storing

Place fresh parsley stalks in water and keep them in the refrigerator for a few days. Dry parsley by cutting it at the base and hanging it up in a shady, warm, well-ventilated area. Once dry, crumble it up and store it in an airtight container.

Try this

Place a handful of fresh parsley into a warm bath to help remedy bruises.

Passionflower *(Passiflora incarnata)*

Hardiness Zone: 5-9

Although it looks like a stunning tropical plant with its wide purple flowers and unique trailing tendencies, passionflower can be grown in many different parts of the country - even cooler areas. Common names for this species of passionflower include maypop, apricot vine, and purple passionflower. This species of passionflower is a beautiful perennial vine that can grow up to 30 feet and spreads by root suckers. It grows quickly, producing edible, light green fruit with a tart apricot flavor that can be made into a tasty drink.

Medicinal properties

Passionflower was commonly used in the 1800s to treat extreme anxiety, as it can slow breathing, which helps lower the pulse and decrease blood pressure. Today it's used for stomach upset related to nerves or anxiety, general anxiety disorder, insomnia, and even easing narcotic drug withdrawal symptoms.

Starting

To aid in germination, pre-soak seeds for 24 hours in warm water. Discard any seeds that float on top of the water as these are not viable. Fill two-inch planting cups with lightweight potting mix and slightly dampen. Plant three seeds per cup, a half-inch deep. Insert pots in zipper bags to create a greenhouse effect - blow lightly into the bag and then seal to trap in moisture. Place pots on top of a heat mat set at 75 degrees F in an area that receives indirect light. Keep planting medium moist. Once seedlings have their third set of leaves, remove the heat mat and the zipper bag and leave the plant to grow in the same location.

Growing tips

Passionflower is a tropical vine that can be grown indoors to create a tropical look inside your home. It prefers temperatures that remain steady between 55 to 65 degrees Fahrenheit; however, it can tolerate slightly cooler temperatures. It likes lots of light, but keep it out of direct sun. Water it regularly while it's growing, providing adequate drainage. For outdoor growing, transplant seedlings into the garden once they reach six inches. Choose a sunny location and space plants about 36 inches apart. Provide a sturdy trellis for climbing or allow the vine to ramble through your garden bed.

Harvesting

When plants are mature and blooming, cut the stems, leaves, and flowers from the plant using clean, sharp scissors.

Storing

Gather the cuttings into a bundle and tie with garden twine. Hang bundles in a sunny window and let them to dry for two weeks. Untie the bundles when they are dry and brittle to touch. Crush the leaves, stems, and flowers and place them in a glass jar with a tight lid. Store the jar in your pantry.

Peppermint *(Mentha x piperita)*

Hardiness Zone: 3-11

Peppermint is synonymous with the Christmas season, and it is also one of the world's most popular and well-loved herbs. It's been used for thousands of years and was even mentioned in the world's oldest surviving medical text, the Ebers Papyrus, which is believed to date back to the 16th-century B.C.E.

Medicinal properties

Throughout history, peppermint has been used to treat various digestive ailments, easing everything from bloating and gas to constipation and diarrhea. Today, many turn to the herbal extract for relief from Irritable Bowel Syndrome (IBS) symptoms. The essential oil of peppermint has been proven to be effective in inhibiting bacterial growth along with certain types of fungal growths.

Peppermint has had a reputation for over 1,000 years for being great at eliminating bad breath by killing odor-causing bacteria, which is why your toothpaste is likely peppermint flavored. The herb is an excellent source of manganese, vitamins C, A, and B2, folate, iron, calcium, and potassium, to name just a few of the nutrients these small but mighty leaves bring to the table. The high concentrations of carotenoids also link the herb very closely with colorectal cancer protection.

Peppermint oil increases alertness and boosts energy without the caffeine, chemicals, and calories of energy drinks, and improves stamina in those with chronic fatigue syndrome. Plus, this oil is a natural topical remedy for eczema and psoriasis. It can even help dry up acne breakouts and balance dry or oily skin, as its antimicrobial properties kill germs while leaving your skin feeling tingly and fresh. Peppermint oil is also effective against nasal allergies when inhaled, clearing the nasal passages of any dust, pollen, and mucus that might be trapped in there. It can relieve blocked sinuses, headaches, sore throats, congestion, and asthma.

Starting

Start seeds indoors six weeks before the last expected frost or wait until springtime and direct sow into the garden. Because seeds germinate best when they are exposed to light, lightly press them into the potting mix and keep the growing medium moist. Seedlings will emerge in 10 to 16 days at room temperature.

The Ancient Greeks thought that peppermint could cure hiccups.

Growing tips

Peppermint is best grown in containers due to its invasive nature, making it ideal for growing indoors or in a small outdoor space like a patio or balcony. It does best in moist, well-drained soil and partial sun. Avoid putting it in a place where it gets lots of full, direct sun. For a lengthy harvest, keep the flowers pinched back, but wait until the plant is 10 to 12 inches high before picking the leaves to avoid weakening. They tend to be at their best just before flowering.

Harvesting

Harvest in the early morning by cutting stems to one inch above the soil line with clean, sharp pruning shears. Discard any damaged, brown, or withered leaves. Alternatively, harvest just a few leaves at a time as needed for tea or other remedies.

Storing

To store fresh peppermint, wrap leaves carefully in a damp paper towel. Place in a plastic zipper bag and seal it well. You can also trim the ends of stems and place them in a glass filled with an inch of water. Cover with a loose-fitting bag and refrigerate. Replace the water when it gets cloudy. Use fresh mint within three to five days of harvesting. Hang bunches upside down in paper bags in an airy, dark place. Leaves will become crumbly in about two weeks. Oven dry with the oven set to 180 degrees F. Spread the leaves on cookie sheets and dry for two to four hours or until crumbly. Store dried mint in an airtight container in the pantry.

You can also make mint ice cups by removing stems and placing two teaspoons of mint into each compartment of a silicone ice cube tray. Top the cubes off with water and freeze. Once frozen, store cubes in a freezer bag or container for three months. Use in your favorite fresh drinks, sauces, teas, or soups.

Try this

Liven up your hot chocolate with fresh mint leaves.
Make your favorite hot cocoa and towards the end
of the steaming process, add clean, torn mint leaves.
Allow them to infuse in the hot chocolate for at
least ten minutes, strain, and enjoy.

Purslane *(Portulaca oleracea)*

Hardiness Zone: 5-10

Purslane, also known as pigweed and pusley, is a small annual succulent plant that creeps its way around meadows, lawns, and gardens. Purslane originates from India, where it was a favored food crop centuries ago. It was reported to be Gandhi's favorite food. To some, including the FDA, purslane is a weed; to others, it is a sensational summer vegetable, a plant full of tremendous health benefits with a mild sweet and sour taste and a delectable texture. Purslane has red stems, fleshy green leaves, and bright yellow flowers.

Medicinal properties

Purslane has the greatest amount of omega-3 fatty acids of all edible plants. This remarkable herb also contains more than 20 times the melatonin found in any other fruit or vegetable. Melatonin is a powerful antioxidant that is thought to protect from cancer. It has also been found to contain analgesic, antibacterial, skeletal muscle-relaxant, and wound-healing properties.

This pretty herb is loaded with vitamin A for optimal vision and keeps the mucus membranes of the skin healthy, potentially protecting against lung and oral cavity cancers. Purslane plants are a rich source of vitamin C and some B-complex vitamins, including magnesium, calcium, iron, potassium, and manganese.

Starting

Although purslane is typically started from seed, you can also grow it from transplants, stem cuttings, and divisions. You will only have to buy purslane seeds once, as one plant produces up to 50,000 seeds throughout its lifetime. Start seeds indoors two weeks before the last frost or direct sow once the soil temperature reaches 60 degrees F. Moisten the soil and sprinkle seeds on top, then press down lightly. Do not cover, as they need light to germinate. In about a week, they should start to sprout. After a few true leaves form, transplant or thin plants to one every eight inches.

Growing tips

Purslane loves full sun, but in very hot areas, it prefers a little afternoon shade to produce big blooms. As far as heat, purslane does best in temperatures above 70 degrees F and even loves it when temperatures skyrocket to over 100 degrees F. Purslane is not picky about soil type as long as it drains well. You will find it growing in cracks on the side of the road and sidewalks. Although purslane does not require fertilizer, adding some compost into the planting soil is a good idea.

Don't overdo it with water - heat-loving plants die if they get too much moisture. To see if your plant needs water, stick your finger into the soil - if dry up to the first knuckle - give a little water. Trim purslane back to two inches above the soil or harvest before it flowers to keep it from taking over your garden. Applying wood chips and mulch can also help reduce spreading. Purslane is also quite happy in containers if you are worried about keeping it contained.

Harvesting

Harvest mature leaves about 50 days after planting seeds. If you harvest in the morning, the leaves contain more malic acid and have a tart taste. Leaves harvested in the evening are sweeter. Snip the plant section you wish to harvest using clean, sharp scissors and place the harvested stems in a cold place. You can harvest one stem - it will grow back - or you can take a whole bunch as long as you leave about two inches of the plant above the soil line.

Storing

Wrap leaves and stems in a cotton cloth and place in the refrigerator for up to one week. Keep in mind; they last a bit longer if you don't wash them immediately after harvesting. Dry using a food dehydrator or oven set at 135 degrees F until they become brittle.

If you are picking wild purslane, be extremely careful of poisonous spurge – it looks similar to purslane but produces a milky sap when it is broken. The stem of spurge is also wiry and not thick like purslane.

Try this

Use dried purslane in your favorite bread recipes and to thicken soups or desserts.

Red Clover *(Trifolium pratense)*

Hardiness Zone: 3-8

Red clover is a wild flowering perennial plant from the same family as peas and beans. It is native to Europe, Asia, and North Africa and grown mainly as forage in many places. Although you may pull lots of clover from your garden beds, it is so much more than an unruly weed. Its beautiful pinkish flowers attract pollinators, and like other legumes, it adds nitrogen to the soil and increases the organic matter, which improves soil structure. This is one reason why it is often used as a cover crop. The flower makes a tasty garnish and can be extracted to produce essential oils.

Medicinal properties

Red clover is rich in minerals, including calcium, nitrogen, and iron, making it a great addition to fresh salads. This sweet plant also contains isoflavones - a type of phytoestrogen and plant compound that can mimic estrogen in the body and may decrease the risk of osteoporosis. Isoflavones also help reduce menopause symptoms like hot flashes, night sweats, anxiety, and vaginal dryness. Extract from red clover has been used in traditional medicine to improve the texture, appearance, and quality of both skin and hair, and it may improve heart health in postmenopausal women. Clover is an expectorant, antispasmodic, and contains sedative and anti-inflammatory properties as well. This explains its ability to relieve symptoms associated with gout, bronchitis, fevers, coughs, and colds.

Starting

Start clover indoors four to six weeks before the last known frost. Sow seeds on top of the planting medium and lightly cover. Transplant outside when the soil is warm, and seedlings have six true leaves. Direct sow by planting seeds a quarter-inch deep and keep them moderately moist until germination, which takes about two to three weeks.

Growing tips

Clover prefers well-draining, slightly acidic soil. It will thrive in full sun or partial shade but is most prolific in full sun. When sowing clover outdoors in your garden, choose the location carefully as it can spread and quickly become invasive.

Harvesting

Blossoms are ready for harvesting between one and two weeks after they first bloom and can be harvested up to three times a season. To harvest red clover, simply pluck off the flower heads and top leaves. For drying, harvest in the early morning when there is still some dew on the flowers, this way, they will not turn brown.

Storing

Place blossoms on a drying rack in a dark, dry, warm, and well-ventilated location. Ensure that there is plenty of space between blossoms and that they are not touching each other. Turn them daily while drying. Clover should be dried within one to two weeks. Store dried blossoms in a jar with a tight-fitting lid.

Try this

For a naturally sweet tea, pour hot water over two teaspoons of red clover and steep for 15 minutes. Add raw honey if extra sweetness is desired.

Rosemary *(Salvia rosmarinus)*

Hardiness Zone: 6-10

Almost everyone is familiar with the woodsy aroma of this native Mediterranean herb that is adorned with needlelike leaves and beautiful blue flowers. Rosemary, a member of the Lamiaceae family of plants, including mint, oregano, lemon balm, and basil, has a rich history of culinary and medicinal use. In fact, many of us would consider rosemary one of our favorite herbs. Who doesn't love recipes like rosemary baked chicken or rosemary potatoes? It's excellent in a wide range of recipes and easy to find at most grocery stores. But rosemary has more to offer than just its tastiness, including a wide range of essential health benefits that affect many parts of the body.

Medicinal properties

Rosemary contains powerful antioxidants that behave like a shield against damaging free radicals that cause oxidative stress and inflammation in the body. Compounds found in rosemary tea have antimicrobial properties that can help your body beat infection and increase glucose absorption into muscle cells to help lower blood sugar.

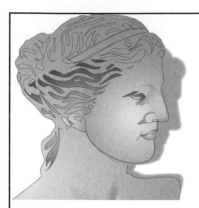

Ancient Greeks associated rosemary with the goddess of fertility, Aphrodite.

Rosemary leaves are used in traditional medicine for their antibacterial and wound healing effects. Therapeutic properties in rosemary can reduce stress and improve mood, partly by improving healthy gut bacteria and reducing inflammation in the part of the brain related to memories and learning. There is also some evidence that rosemary can help offset the negative impacts of brain aging and help protect the brain from neurodegenerative conditions like Alzheimer's.

Starting

Rosemary seeds have a very low germination rate, making stem cuttings a great way to start plants. Choose healthy stems from a mature mother plant. Young shoots are flexible and green, do not choose older brown or woody stems.

Growing tips

Plant rosemary in the spring once the temperature has warmed up and the threat of frost has passed. This aromatic herb is happy in raised garden beds, containers, and in-ground gardens. Allow for two feet between plants and choose a location that receives plenty of sunshine and has rich, well-draining soil. For best results, mix a few inches of compost into planting soil and feed regularly with an organic fertilizer. Although it is essential to water rosemary regularly, do not do so unless the soil is dry. Growing rosemary indoors can be tricky, and even experienced gardeners end up with dead plants despite their best efforts. Still, it is possible to do as long as your plants can get plenty of sunlight, proper watering, and a room with good air circulation.

Harvesting

Use clean, sharp garden shears to harvest stems from mature plants. Do not take more than one-third of the plant each time you harvest.

Storing

If you wish to use fresh rosemary within two weeks of harvest, store it in the refrigerator. Wrap sprigs in a damp paper towel and place them in a container or a zipper bag. Freezing rosemary allows you to use it later. Rinse off sprigs and let them dry, cut sprigs six to eight inches long, and place them in a freezer-safe bag. You can also fill ice cube tray slots halfway with rosemary pieces, cover with water and freeze. Once frozen, place the cubes in a freezer bag and store them for up to six months. Although dried rosemary is not as aromatic as fresh rosemary, it lasts for several years when properly stored. Place sprigs on a plate and set them in a dry location for a few days. After they have dried, remove the leaves and stems and store them in a sealed container. You can also grind rosemary into a fine powder using a mortar and pestle.

Try this

Add some dried rosemary to your favorite shortbread cookie recipe. You will love the added taste, texture, and color that rosemary brings.

Sage *(Salvia officinalis)*

Hardiness Zone: 5-8

Sage is a hardy perennial plant with attractive grayish-green leaves and pretty spikes of purple, blue, white, and pink flowers. It is known by several names, including common sage and garden sage, and is a member of the mint family. Sage has a potent aroma and earthy flavor and is often used in small amounts in bread, pasta, salad, soup, and sauce. It even adds a wonderful fragrant earthiness to desserts. Sage is also employed as a natural cleaning agent, natural pesticide, and in ritual cleansing with sage burning.

Medicinal properties

Sage is an outstanding source of fiber, vitamin A, folate, calcium, iron, magnesium, manganese, and B vitamins. When made into a tea, this earthy herb effectively relieves digestive ailments like bloating and gas. It may also help improve memory, brain function, mood, attention span, and LDL cholesterol. Sage contains both antioxidant and anti-inflammatory properties and has been found to remedy excessive sweating, vertigo, and hypotension. When applied to the skin, fresh sage can take the itch and sting out of insect bites because of its astringent and antiseptic properties. It can also be used in mouthwash to effectively kill the bacteria *Streptococcus mutans* that causes cavities. Compounds in sage contain estrogen-like properties, which help reduce hot flashes and brain fog associated with menopause. Some evidence suggests that sage extract can lower blood sugar and reduce wrinkles and other signs of skin aging.

Starting

Start seeds indoors six weeks before the last known frost—cover seeds lightly with potting mix. Germination takes between 10 to 21 days. Transplant seedlings when they have two sets of true leaves and are about four inches tall. Space plants 18 inches apart in the garden or containers.

Growing tips

Sage needs lots of sun and loves hot weather. If you grow it indoors, be sure to place it in a sunny window sill, as it provides the tastiest leaves when it gets lots of sunlight. Choose well-drained, loamy, sandy soil with a pH of 6.0 to 7.0, and wait until the soil dries out before giving it a thorough watering.

Harvesting

Where sage is grown as a perennial, harvest lightly the first year and, after that, harvest as needed. Pinch off individual leaves or cut the entire stem. Leave at least two months between large harvests to allow the plant time to recover. Otherwise, when grown as an annual or in containers, pinch off leaves as needed.

Storing

Wrap sage leaves in paper towels and put them in a zipper bag in the refrigerator. They will keep for up to five days this way. Leaves covered in olive oil last in the refrigerator for several weeks. You can also freeze the leaves by washing and drying them and packing them loosely in a freezer bag where they should last for up to a year. Another way to store sage for the long term is to dry it by hanging bunches upside down in a dry location. Once dry, strip the leaves from the stem and store them in a container with a tight-fitting lid.

Try this

Toss a handful of fresh sage leaves into a warm bath to relieve muscle pain and reduce sciatic pain and inflammation.

Spearmint *(Mentha spicata)*

Hardiness Zone: 3-11

Spearmint is a mint, like peppermint, and is a perennial herb
from Europe and Asia. Most people are familiar with the flavor of
spearmint from gum or toothpaste. Spearmint grows up to two feet
tall and wide and has dark green leaves that contain the flavor and
fragrance. The small flowers that bloom in late summer grow in
spikes and are white, pink, or lavender. Mentions of spearmint date
back nearly 2,000 years, but people in the Mediterranean likely used
mint plants much earlier than that.

Medicinal properties

Spearmint has a refreshing, cooling flavor and aroma, but it also has medicinal properties. Historically, people used spearmint for stomach ailments and to clean the teeth and freshen the mouth. These uses continue today, but research has shown that spearmint has many other benefits. For instance, researchers have isolated a compound in spearmint that inhibits digestive muscle contractions, explaining how it works to settle upset stomachs. Some other potential benefits of spearmint include balancing hormones, improving memory, lowering blood sugar, reducing stress, and treating bacterial infections.

Starting

Start spearmint seeds indoors about eight weeks before the last spring frost. Use high-quality potting soil and cover the seeds to a depth of a quarter inch. Keep the soil moist and warm, and expect the seeds to sprout within one to two weeks. Make sure the seedlings get plenty of sunlight.

Growing tips

Mint plants tend to overtake areas where they grow, spreading underground by rhizomes. To keep spearmint under control, it's best to grow plants in containers. You can grow spearmint inside or outside. It will grow well in full sun but also tolerate partial shade; however, it does need regular water, so don't let the soil dry out completely. Mulch can help keep it moist and deter weeds if growing outside.

Harvesting

You can pick off leaves of spearmint as needed. You can also take off entire stems of leaves. Use shears or scissors to avoid damaging the plant. The leaves are best before the plant flowers. Just before the flowers appear, you can cut all the stems back to about an inch from the ground for a total harvest. This will encourage new growth, and you may get a second harvest in the same season.

Storing

Use fresh spearmint leaves for cooking or making drinks. You can store them in the crisper in the refrigerator for a few days. Also, try placing stems in a glass of water to keep them fresh a little longer. To store a large harvest, let the leaves dry. Spread them out on a drying screen in a spot shielded from light and wind. Store the crushed, dried leaves in an airtight container.

Try this

Spearmint tea is easy to make and is an effective remedy for an upset stomach. Steep a teaspoon of dried, crushed leaves in a cup of boiling water for five minutes. Strain to drink. If using fresh leaves, pair a large handful with two cups of water. Make spearmint iced tea for a relaxing, stomach-soothing drink on hot days.

St John's Wort *(Hypericum perforatum)*

Hardiness Zone: 5-10

If any plant would have an identity crisis, it would be St. John's Wort. It is a noxious weed to some, a beautiful wildflower to others, and a powerful natural medicine to those who embrace the healing power of the garden. The truth is, it can be all things, as the eye is truly in the beholder. However, this European native does make a fantastic addition to any medicinal plant garden. It is a mid-size perennial with a shrub-like growing habit that generally tops out at three feet tall. It is decorated with yellow flowers from midsummer until fall, followed up by colorful berries. This hardy plant is not picky about soil and is often used as a ground cover to stabilize the soil.

Medicinal properties

This herb contains dozens of biologically active compounds. Hyperforin, hypericin, and adhyperforin appear to offer the most medicinal punch. They increase levels of chemical messengers in the brain, including dopamine, serotonin, and noradrenaline, which may account for its anti-depressive capabilities in people with moderate depression. Additionally, St. John's wort relieves PMS symptoms, fights inflammatory conditions including skin rashes, bruises, and bumps, and even reduces the risk of cancer. Powerful antiviral compounds encourage wound healing.

Starting

Seeds require a period of cold, moist conditions for optimal germination - place in the fridge three to four weeks before planting. Because seeds need light to germinate, press them lightly into the soil. Germination occurs in about two weeks. Start indoors four to six weeks before the last anticipated spring frost or direct sow in the springtime—thin seedlings when planting so that there is one plant every 12 inches.

Growing tips

Keep new plants moist for at least a year until they are well established. After this, plants require just a couple of inches of water per week to thrive. Growing St. John's wort is fairly easy, though it's best done outdoors in a location that gets bright morning sunlight and partial shade in the hottest part of the afternoon. Too much shade will reduce the number of flowers it produces, but too much sun can cause leaf scorch. To prevent it from smothering other plants, you may want to grow it in containers. Use nutrient-rich soil and add a layer of mulch around the base to keep moisture in.

Harvesting

Pick fresh flowers and buds or cut off the top three inches of the plant when it is in full bloom.

St. John's Wort gets its name from the fact that it often blooms on the birthday of the biblical figure John the Baptist.

Storing

It is best to use flowers and buds when fresh, not dried, as they are not as potent. Use it when fresh to make oil, tinctures, teas, or salve. If you do wish to dry, spread flowers on a screen in a cool, dark place.

Try this

Make a delicious tea with a lemony taste by steeping three teaspoons of fresh flowers in hot water for four minutes. Strain, add local raw honey to sweeten, and enjoy.

Stevia *(Stevia rebaudiana)*

Hardiness zone: 10-11

Stevia is well known today as a nonnutritive sweetener - basically a sugar substitute. You can buy powdered stevia products to add sweetness to foods and drinks without adding calories. These products contain rebaudioside A, an extract made from stevia leaves. A more natural way to sweeten foods without calories is to use the whole leaves of the stevia plant.

Stevia, part of the Asteraceae family, is an herbaceous perennial that grows up to two feet tall and wide. Native to South America, this plant can be grown indoors year-round or outdoors in summer. It has little ornamental value, but stevia does produce small white flowers in late summer.

Medicinal properties

The native people of Brazil and Paraguay have used this plant for thousands of years to sweeten drinks and make medicines more palatable. The known health benefits of stevia are related to calorie intake and weight loss or maintenance. Studies have found that using stevia can help people with diabetes manage blood sugar levels. One study also found that stevia can reduce bad cholesterol levels. If the use of stevia reduces your sugar intake, it can help you lose or maintain weight. A few studies have found that stevia may have anti-cancer properties as well.

Starting

Because it is a tropical plant, it's best to start stevia seeds indoors eight to ten weeks before the last frost. Sow seeds to a depth of a quarter-inch and look for seedlings to emerge in two to three weeks. Keep the starting soil lightly moist and give the seedlings plenty of sun or artificial light.

Growing tips

Grow transplants outdoors in a spot with full sun and average soil. If you do not live in a warm, tropical climate, you may want to grow stevia in containers. You can keep the plants outside in the summer and bring them in again for the winter. Pinch off the tips of the plants every few weeks to give them a fuller growth shape. Water regularly, but don't let the soil get soggy. You can use a standard plant fertilizer throughout the growing season.

Harvesting

Harvest stevia leaves as you need them. They have the best flavor before flowering, so pinch off flowers as they begin to appear. Alternatively, you can harvest the entire plant by pulling it up just before flowering.

Storing

Use stevia leaves fresh in teas and other beverages. You can store the fresh leaves in the refrigerator for a few days or in a glass of water. To keep the leaves for longer use, dry them. Hang stems or lay leaves out on a drying screen. Store in an airtight container.

Try this

Make a stevia syrup to add to drinks. Pulverize dried stevia leaves until nearly a powder. Use a mortar and pestle or blender to do this. Add one teaspoon to two cups of boiling water. Simmer until it achieves a thick, syrup-like consistency. Strain out the stevia and store the syrup in the refrigerator.

Stinging Nettles *(Urtica dioica)*

Hardiness Zone: 3–10

Stinging nettles probably doesn't sound like a plant you'd want to have in your garden, as its tiny, acid-filled nettles cause a painful rash when you touch the leaves with your bare skin. Fortunately, the nettles on these fast-growing plants fall off after you boil them. These boiled leaves are totally safe and provide magnesium, potassium, iodine, and phosphorus, along with a wide range of medicinal benefits. This distant cousin to mint is loaded with health-promoting properties, making it a popular choice for any medicinal garden. As a bonus, its plant fibers can be woven into a cloth equal in quality to flax and hemp-based fabrics.

Medicinal properties

Stinging nettles has the power to strengthen the immune system, regulate menstruation, improve energy and circulation, protect the kidneys, reduce inflammation, lower blood pressure, and improve respiratory disorders. Leaves are rich in antioxidants, and according to the USDA, nettle leaf powder is one of the richest sources of minerals among all edible plants. There is evidence that this plant contains blood-sugar-lowering compounds that mimic insulin. Creams made with nettles help encourage the healing of wounds and burns. Some cultures make nettle soup or add it to cheese, though stinging nettle leaves are most commonly used to brew tea.

Starting

Stinging nettles are best grown from seeds started indoors and then grown outdoors in containers or directly in your garden. Start seeds about four to six weeks before the last anticipated spring frost. Plant three seeds in each start pot filled with potting mix and then lightly cover them with about a quarter-inch of soil. Keep them moist, and in about two weeks, they should germinate. Direct sow in the garden in rich, moist soil in an area away from other herbs. Sow in rows, placing seeds about 12 inches apart, and be sure to keep seeds moist until germination.

Growing tips

These prolific growers can reach up to four or five feet tall pretty quickly. Keep seeds moist with regular watering, but avoid excessive moisture.

If you do happen to get stung by a nettle, make a paste with apple cider vinegar, baking soda, and water and place it on the sting.

Harvesting

Start harvesting using sharp garden scissors after about 90 days from seed planting. Leaves are most tender in the first few weeks of spring, but you can harvest through summer, snipping off the top few pairs of leaves each time. Wear gloves and a long sleeve shirt and pants when you harvest to protect your skin. Place harvested material in a paper bag or a bucket. The good news is, the hollow trichomes that cause itching will deflate soon after harvest, but gloves are still recommended.

Storing

Fresh nettles store well unwashed in a sealable bag in the refrigerator's vegetable drawer for a few days. Be sure to rinse before use. There are several ways to dry nettles for tea and other formulations. Use an oven set at a low temperature or a food dehydrator. To freeze, run raw plant material through a food processor until finely chopped. Place in freezer-proof containers.

Try this

Substitute stinging nettles for spinach in any recipe. Add it to pasta, soups, stews, or even lasagna.

Sunflower *(Helianthus annuus)*

Hardiness Zone: 4-9

Sunflower is an annual native to parts of North America that was cultivated as a crop by Native Americans. Over thousands of years, these native people developed a flower with a large seed head and used the seeds as a food source, eating them raw, roasted, dried, and as an oil.

Most people picture the tall, yellow flowers with brown centers when thinking about sunflowers, but they come in various sizes and colors. They can be as short as 16 inches and come in shades of yellow, red, brown, and even white and striped.

Medicinal properties

Most parts of the sunflower are edible and nutritious, including the petals, roots, and stalks. The seeds and sprouts, in particular, contain a lot of nutrients, including antioxidants and anti-inflammatory properties. Native Americans used sunflowers for several medicinal purposes: to treat kidney disease, to treat respiratory infections, to stimulate the appetite, to lower fevers, and to treat skin conditions and snake bites.

Starting

Sunflowers grow fast, maturing in just 85 to 95 days, so there is no need to start seeds indoors. Sow seeds right in the ground after the risk of a spring frost has passed or when the soil is at least 50 degrees. Because they have deep roots, prepare the soil to a depth of two feet. The spot should be sunny and must drain well. Sow the seeds six inches apart and one inch deep.

Growing tips

You can grow smaller, shorter varieties of sunflower in containers or even indoors. For the taller types, grow directly in the ground outside. Water sunflowers deeply and infrequently to encourage deep root growth. For the tallest varieties, you may need to stake the flowers, especially if you live in a windy area. Use fertilizer sparingly, as too much will cause stems to weaken and break.

Harvesting

Harvest leaves at any time to use for medicinal preparations. Remove the flower bud to prepare and eat as you would an artichoke. To harvest the seeds, let the flower dry on the plant. The seeds are usually ready when the back of the flower head is brown and the leaves are yellow. Cut the head off and shake the seeds out over a tray. You may need to rub them loose.

Storing

Dry and store leaves in airtight containers for medicinal use. To store seeds, soak them in water overnight and then spread them out on a paper towel to dry. Bake the seeds in a single layer in an oven at 325 degrees Fahrenheit. Stir a few times as they bake and store the seeds in a container for a few weeks.

Try this

Make a poultice of sunflower leaves to treat a fever and skin ailments, like sores, inflammation, and insect bites. Cut fresh leaves into small pieces and then crush them until they form a paste. A mortar and pestle works well if you have one. If not, use a blender. Spread the paste onto the affected area and wrap with gauze.

Tarragon *(Artemisia dracunculus)*

Hardiness Zone: 2-9

There are two well-known varieties of tarragon, Russian *(Artemisia dracunculoides)* and French *(Artemisia dracunculus var. sativa)*. The most common variety used in cooking is French tarragon, with a delicate flavor that pairs well with eggs, chicken, and fish. It is often referred to by the French as "the king of herbs" because it can elevate a dish to great heights.

This leafy green plant from the sunflower and daisy family also has powerful medicinal properties. It has an appealing flavor similar to anise and licorice and makes a beautiful border plant with its delicate upright leaves and sweet fragrance. Russian tarragon is known as "false" tarragon and is similar in shape and appearance to the French variety, but it has a bitter taste and musty aroma. The following cultivation information refers to the French variety.

Medicinal properties

Tarragon is a great source of minerals like calcium, zinc, magnesium, and iron, and it is rich in vitamin A, B-6, and C. It also offers antioxidants that help battle excess free radicals that can lead to cellular damage and a host of diseases. Tarragon is known to support heart health and digestion, and it can lower blood sugar levels as well. The Artemisia group of plants, including tarragon, has sedative properties and has been used as a remedy for insomnia and to regulate sleep patterns. There is pressure being put on food manufacturers to use natural preservatives, and tarragon essential oil ranks at the top of the list since it can fight off bacteria that causes foodborne illness.

Ancient Greeks chewed on tarragon leaves to numb their mouth and to alleviate tooth pain. This pain relief came from a high concentration of eugenol found in the herb.

Starting

Unlike Russian tarragon, French tarragon can't be started by seed. It can only be started by stem cuttings or root division. For cuttings, take them from young stems in the morning. Cut a four to eight-inch piece of stem below a node and remove the lower one-third of leaves. Dip the end into rooting hormone and plant it in a container filled with warm, moist potting soil. Keep the new plant well misted daily, and once roots form, you can transplant it into the garden after the threat of frost has passed. Space plants two feet apart to give them plenty of room to thrive.

Growing tips

Tarragon can grow up to three feet tall with a 12-15 inch spread and prefers moderate sun with a little shade during the hottest part of the day. This aromatic herb is not fussy about soil and will thrive in areas with poor, dry, and even sandy conditions once established. Provide mulch to keep moisture locked in near the soil surface. Prune to shape and divide larger plants in the spring to keep them healthy. When the leaves on the plant turn yellow as cooler weather approaches, cut the plant back, leaving only four inches above the crown. This ensures that energy can be diverted back to the roots in preparation for next year's growth. Tarragon is happy indoors in a container as long as you provide at least six hours of sunlight per day and fertilize with a diluted fish fertilizer every two weeks.

Harvesting

Harvest leaves from established plants in the morning when essential oils are strongest. Keep harvesting until late August, and be sure to stop harvesting one month before the first fall frost date in your growing zone. Always leave at least one-third of the foliage on the plant and use sharp, clean shears to harvest, not your hands. Snip newer, light-green leaves first or an entire branch.

Storing

Use fresh leaves immediately or store them in a freezer bag. To keep an entire sprig fresh, place it in a glass of water. Dry tarragon by hanging the shoots in a cool, dry space. Once dry, store in a container with a tight-fitting lid or in a zipper bag.

Try this

Toss a few tarragon leaves into your favorite salad to amp up your greens and delight your tastebuds.

Thyme *(Thymus vulgaris)*

Hardiness Zone: 5-9

Thyme is a Mediterranean perennial herb with a wonderful aroma and distinctly sweet taste. There are over 50 thyme varieties that all belong to the mint family. Thymus vulgaris is often referred to as common thyme or garden thyme and is a woody perennial with a low growing habit, aromatic leaves, and edible lavender-colored flowers that attract bees and make it an excellent border plant. Its drought-tolerant nature makes it an easy grower. French and lemon thyme are popular culinary varieties.

Medicinal properties

This popular garden herb offers a host of therapeutic benefits thanks to its antibacterial and antifungal properties. Centuries ago, it was used for embalming and to theoretically protect people from the Black Death. Thyme essential oil and thymol (a significant constituent of thyme oil) are suitable weapons against low concentrations of mold. The flowers, leaves, and oil of thyme have all been found to lower high blood pressure and treat many other conditions, from a sore throat, cough, and bronchitis, to arthritis, diarrhea, and colic. Thyme is loaded with vitamin C and is also a good source of vitamin A to help boost your immunity. Findings have been impressive in studies using thyme tinctures to fight acne, as it has been found to perform better than commonly prescribed acne medication.

Starting

Because it is hard to grow thyme from seeds, try taking cuttings from a friend's plant or buy a new plant from a reputable garden nursery. Start cuttings indoors six to 10 weeks before the last spring frost and transplant into a sunny, well-draining spot in the garden after the temperature reaches a steady 70 degrees. Space plants about 18 inches apart or grow in containers.

Growing tips

Thyme can be grown indoors, and it thrives in pots that are as small as just four to six inches. It prefers light, fast-draining soil, along with full sun. East-facing window sills are generally a good spot for success. Water thyme regularly, but be careful not to overwater. It's naturally drought resistant and does best when the soil is allowed to become slightly dry between waterings. Prune plants in the spring and summer to control growth. Mulch in areas where the ground freezes and prune every three years to encourage full growth.

Harvesting

Harvest just as the plant begins to flower and in the morning after the dew has dried. Use clean, sharp garden scissors to cut the top five inches of growth - leaving the woody parts.

Storing

If the leaves are clean, don't wash them, as this removes some of the essential plant oil—store fresh thyme lightly wrapped in plastic for two weeks in the refrigerator. To dry, hang the sprigs in a dark, warm, airy space. You can also employ a food dehydrator. Once dry, store in an airtight container and crush just before using. When dried, thyme will hold its flavor for up to two years. Freeze freshly cut thyme by placing small pieces in ice cube trays. Cover with water and transfer to freezer bags once frozen.

Try this

Make a soothing cinnamon and thyme tea when you are feeling under the weather. Bring four cups of water to a boil and add four teaspoons of dried thyme and two cinnamon sticks. Let the tea steep for 15 minutes and strain into a quart-size Mason jar. Sweeten with local raw honey.

Valerian *(Valeriana officinalis)*

Hardiness Zone: 4-9

Valerian is a perennial herb native to Europe and naturalized in
North America that was used in ancient Greece and Rome as a
sleep aid. It grows up to five feet tall in clumps with large basal
leaves and fewer leaves higher on the stems. In mid-summer,
valerian blooms into white or pink flowers on panicles. The leaves
and flowers are highly fragrant. The roots are also fragrant and are
used for medicinal preparations.

Medicinal properties

Historically, people used valerian to treat insomnia, headaches, stomach cramps, and fatigue. Today, people use valerian preparations for insomnia, anxiety, depression, menopause, headaches, and PMS. Research into valerian is limited but has uncovered compounds that may reduce anxiety and promote sleep by interacting with a neurotransmitter in the brain known as GABA. There is some evidence that valerian can help ease anxiety, but results are mixed. Research also backs up the use of valerian for better sleep. However, there are some potential side effects, and valerian may interfere with some medications and medical conditions, so it's best to talk to your doctor before using it.

Starting

Grow valerian from seed or transplants. Sow seeds indoors about four weeks before the last frost. Use standard starting soil and sow to a depth of three-eighths of an inch. Transplant outside 18 inches apart when the danger of frost is past.

Growing tips

Valerian grows well in a range of soil types, but moist, loamy soil is best. Make sure the spot drains well and is either in full sun or just a little shade. Valerian needs regular watering until it is well established. It will then grow readily without much intervention, so fertilizer isn't necessary. Valerian grows and self-seeds vigorously, and it will readily take over garden spaces. For this reason, you may want to remove flowers before they go to seed or grow the herb in containers. You can grow valerian indoors in large containers with sunny windows.

Harvesting

If you like the smell, you can use cut valerian flowers in arrangements. Keep in mind, it has a strong smell that is not to everyone's taste. For medicinal preparations, harvest the roots. Dig them up in the fall of the second year of growth once the foliage has yellowed.

Storing

Valerian root is used dried in medicinal preparations. Wash roots thoroughly as they are thin and spindly and carry a lot of dirt. You may need to rinse them multiple times. Dry the roots in a food dehydrator or an oven at a low setting. Break up the roots into small pieces. You can use a blender for this or do it by hand. Store dried roots in an airtight container.

Try this

A cup of valerian root tea is an easy way to get the herb's anti-anxiety benefits and sleep benefits. Use a teaspoon of dried root in a cup of water, steep for a full 10 minutes, and strain the root out to drink. Use it about 30 to 60 minutes before bed for insomnia.

Yarrow *(Achillea millefolium)*

Hardiness zone: 3-9

Yarrow is an herb and perennial native to North America, Europe, and parts of Asia. In North America, it grows vigorously enough to be considered a weed by many. Yarrow grows up to three feet tall and has fern-like leaves with small flowers that bloom in dense, flat groups throughout summer. Though the flowers are usually white, you may also find cultivars in red, pink, yellow, and other colors.

Medicinal properties

Yarrow has long been used in traditional medicine. Since ancient times it has been used as an astringent and tonic for gastrointestinal issues, earaches, colds, pain relief, wounds, and fever. Modern studies have found that yarrow may actually be beneficial in some of these ways. There is evidence, for instance, that yarrow can help wounds heal faster, possibly due to anti-inflammatory effects and the stimulation of coagulation. Research also indicates that yarrow can help reduce digestive problems, inflammation, and even anxiety and depression.

Starting

To start yarrow from seed, sow indoors six to eight weeks before the last frost of spring. Use standard potting soil and sow seeds by placing them on the surface of the soil. Yarrow seeds need light to germinate. Set the starting tray in a warm, sunny window.

Growing tips

Plant yarrow transplants outside after the danger of frost has passed or grow them in containers. Give them one or two feet of space in a spot with full sun. The soil should drain very well. Yarrow will not tolerate soil that stays moist, so water only when conditions are dry. A little organic matter in the soil is adequate to feed yarrow as it does not like soil that is too fertile. As flowers fade in midsummer, cut them off to encourage another round of blooms.

Harvesting

To use yarrow medicinally, harvest both the leaves and flowers. To harvest, cut off entire stems when the flowers are blooming. They should be fully open but not yet in decline. Remove the flower cluster and the leaves and discard the stems.

Storing

Fresh yarrow leaves are useful for making a poultice to apply to the skin. To keep yarrow longer and to make medicinal tea, dry both the flowers and leaves. The easiest way to do this is to hang harvested stems until they dry then remove the leaves and flowers, discarding the stems. Crush the flowers and leaves and store them in airtight containers.

Try this

A poultice of yarrow for treating wounds is easy to make and use. Take fresh leaves and crush them to release the juices. You can crush the leaves by hand or use a mortar and pestle. Apply the crushed leaves to the wound and wrap the area with gauze to hold them in place.

Using Medicinal Plants for Wellness

Here are just some ways that plants grown in your backyard pharmacy can be used for health and wellbeing. Remember, once you have a handle on plant properties, the sky's the limit - create your own remedies and have fun doing it!

Essential Oils

Essential oils are highly concentrated extracts obtained from flowers, berries, seeds, gums, roots, bark, needles, or resins of numerous plants. They contain powerful and natural hormones, antibiotics, vitamins, and antiseptics.

Also known as volatile oils, because they evaporate quickly in the air, essential oils can irritate the mucous membranes of the stomach lining if they are taken internally, so it is best to avoid ingesting them. A few drops in bathwater, a diffuser, inhalants, poultices, or on the skin (with a carrier oil) is usually all that is necessary.

Making your own essential oils

Crafting your own essential oils is not as difficult as you may think. Because they can be expensive to purchase, learning how to make your own can save you a lot of money in the long run. Plus, it is something new and fun to try.

The typical method for extracting volatile (essential) oils from plants is steam distillation. You can purchase a copper two-quart still for just under $500, but that is still quite an investment. The good news is, you don't need an expensive still to extract oils successfully.

Most essential oil recipes found online are really infused oils. It is quite essential to know the difference between them. We will get to a few infused oil recipes below, but it is important to note that infused oils are made by soaking herbs in oil to extract their active compounds. While this process works well for some plants like calendula, it does not do as well for others like lavender. Essential oils, on the other hand, are actually just herbs distilled into oil form.

Once you get the hang of making your own oils, you can start to experiment with unique blends.

Making Essential oils:

WHAT YOU NEED

- ☐ **Crockpot with a lid**
- ☐ **Distilled water**
- ☐ **Fresh chopped plant material to fill the crockpot halfway**

HOW TO DO IT

1 Put the chopped plant material in the crockpot and cover it ¾ full with distilled water. Place the lid on upside down.

2 Set the pot to high to heat the water. Once the water is hot, turn it to low and simmer for 3-4 hours.

3 Turn off the pot and let the water cool. Once cool, place the inner container in your pot in the refrigerator for 24 hours.

4 When you remove the crockpot, you will notice a thin film of oil on the top - it will be hard. Very carefully lift it off the water.

5 Quickly scoop what you have taken off the top into a bottle and put a lid on it.

6 If there is a little water on the bottom of the bottle, you can heat the oil briefly to turn it to steam and release it from the oil. Be very careful, though, as heating the oil too long will cause it to become less potent.

7 Store in a dark-colored container away from light and heat.

Lavender Sunscreen

This non-toxic sun barrier is creamy, moisturizing, and easy on your skin.

WHAT YOU NEED

- ☐ 3 drops lavender essential oil
- ☐ 3 drops helichrysum essential oil
- ☐ ½ cup warmed coconut oil
- ☐ ¼ cup whipped shea butter
- ☐ 4 Tbsp zinc oxide

HOW TO MAKE IT

1 Combine the ingredients in a bowl, making sure to mix well.

2 Scooop into tins and store in the refrigerator.

3 Apply as needed.

Peppermint Anti-Nausea Rub

Peppermint is well known for its anti-nausea properties. Apply a few drops to the inside of your wrists when you start feeling queasy.

WHAT YOU NEED

- ☐ **10 drops peppermint essential oil**
- ☐ **10 drops lemon essential oil**
- ☐ **10 drops fennel essential oil**
- ☐ **Sweet almond oil**
- ☐ **Funnel**
- ☐ **Small dropper or roller bottle**

HOW TO MAKE IT

1 Fill the bottle with almond oil and add essential oils.

2 Shake well to combine.

3 Use as needed and store in a cool, dark place.

Sleep Tight Pillow Spray

Sleep well with this relaxing pillow spray. A few pumps before bedtime will usher you into a peaceful dreamland in no time.

WHAT YOU NEED

- ☐ 2 Tbsp witch hazel
- ☐ 2 Tbsp distilled water
- ☐ 10 drops lavender essential oil
- ☐ 10 drops chamomile essential oil
- ☐ 10 drops rose essential oil
- ☐ Amber spray bottle
- ☐ Funnel

HOW TO MAKE IT

1 Combine all ingredients in a small dish and funnel into a mister bottle.

2 Use each evening on your pillow.

Sweet Sugar Scrub

This gentle sugar scrub will leave your skin feeling calm, soft, and supple. Use a couple of times a week and follow up with your favorite moisturizer.

WHAT YOU NEED

- ☐ **20 drops chamomile essential oil**
- ☐ **1 cup white or coconut sugar**
- ☐ **1 Tbsp calendula infused oil**
- ☐ **½ cup coconut oil**

HOW TO MAKE IT

1 Combine all ingredients and place in a container with a lid.

2 Apply in circular motions in the shower, rinse and pat dry.

Green Tea and Mint Hair Refresher

Washing your hair daily can strip it of natural oils that are necessary for healthy locks. This refresher is a perfect pick-me-up anytime you want to give your hair that just-washed feeling. Peppermint oil stimulates hair growth, while tea tree oil helps banish bacteria, and green tea fuels your locks with powerful antioxidants.

WHAT YOU NEED

- ☐ ¼ cup green tea
- ☐ ½ cup distilled water
- ☐ 2 drops apple mint essential oil
- ☐ 1 tsp argan oil
- ☐ 1 tsp tea tree essential oil
- ☐ Spray bottle

HOW TO MAKE IT

1 Combine the ingredients and pour into a spray bottle.

2 Store in the refrigerator for 5 days.

3 Shake and use as needed - spritzing close to your scalp and brushing through your hair.

Cucumber and Aloe Face Mist

Cucumber and aloe are both extremely hydrating and full of vitamins and minerals. Aloe vera can ease irritation and reduce inflammation while refreshing the skin.

WHAT YOU NEED

- ☐ 1 small cucumber
- ☐ ½ cup distilled water
- ☐ 1 tsp aloe vera gel
- ☐ 1 tsp rose water
- ☐ 1 tsp witch hazel
- ☐ Spray bottle

HOW TO MAKE IT

1 Peel and dice cucumber. Put the majority in a food processor and process.

2 Strain the extract through a cheesecloth, wringing out all excess water. Toss any pulp.

3 Combine all ingredients and funnel into a spray bottle.

4 Store in the refrigerator for a cooling mist whenever you need a little pick-me-up.

Apple Cider and Oregano Wart Dissolve

If you are looking for a natural way to remove a wart (a small, benign growth on the skin caused by a virus), this is it. Apple cider vinegar contains powerful acid and probiotics, and the main compounds in oregano essential oil, carvacrol and thymol, both have beneficial antiviral properties. Lemon oil is highly therapeutic as well, and frankincense oil has both disinfectant and antiseptic properties. The addition of coconut oil elevates this solution even further with its antimicrobial and antifungal properties.

WHAT YOU NEED

- ☐ ½ tsp apple cider vinegar
- ☐ 1 drop oregano essential oil
- ☐ 2 drops frankincense essential oil
- ☐ 2 drops lemon essential oil
- ☐ ½ tsp coconut oil, warmed
- ☐ 1 cotton pad
- ☐ 1 bandage

HOW TO MAKE IT

1 Combine the apple cider vinegar and essential oils in a small dish. Mix well.

2 Add the coconut oil and stir to make sure all ingredients are combined.

3 Clean and dry the affected area and use a cotton pad to apply the mixture - soak it slightly before applying.

4 Cover the affected area with a bandage.

5 Apply twice a day as needed.

Sleepless Night Roller

Lemon balm has a long history of being used to ease nervous system disorders. Its soothing properties calm the mind and prepare you for a restful night's sleep. Just keep the roller bottle next to your bed and use it to help you fall asleep. This formula is also great for kids who wake up with bad dreams or have trouble falling asleep.

WHAT YOU NEED

- ☐ **Fractionated coconut oil**
- ☐ **10 drops lemon balm essential oil**
- ☐ **15 drops lavender essential oil**
- ☐ **10 ml glass roller bottle**

HOW TO MAKE IT

1 Measure the essential oil into the bottle and top off with fractionated coconut oil.

2 Put the roller back on and shake well.

Hot Flash Spray

Studies have shown that hot flashes can be brought on by stress and anxiety. Spray this supercharged hot flash-be-gone mixture on your neck, arms, legs, and anywhere else you need relief.

WHAT YOU NEED

- ☐ **2 Tbsp filtered water**
- ☐ **2 Tbsp witch hazel**
- ☐ **15 drops rosemary essential oil**
- ☐ **15 drops roman chamomile essential oil**
- ☐ **15 drops spearmint essential oil**
- ☐ **2 oz glass spray bottle**

HOW TO MAKE IT

1 Place essential oils into the glass spray bottle.

2 Add the water and the witch hazel and shake well.

3 Use this spray at the first sign of a hot flash.

4 You can also use it as a preventative by spraying it on your skin every morning and night.

Peppermint and Rosemary Shampoo

With so many excellent benefits, this easy-to-make natural shampoo will soon be a favorite in your home. As an added benefit, the cost is minimal compared to conventional hair products.

WHAT YOU NEED

- ☐ ½ cup castile soap
- ☐ ½ cup filtered water
- ☐ 15 drops peppermint essential oil
- ☐ 20 drops rosemary essential oil
- ☐ Pump type bottle or bottle of your choice

HOW TO MAKE IT

1 Combine the ingredients in the bottle. Shake well.

2 Use 3 times a week and follow with your favorite natural conditioner. Enjoy!

Puffy Eye Serum

For those sleepy mornings after a late night out or all day staring at a computer screen, this serum will help give your eyes the refresher that they need. Pair with a cooling eye mask, and your tired eyes will thank you.

WHAT YOU NEED

- ☐ **5 drops lavender essential oil**
- ☐ **5 drops lemon essential oil**
- ☐ **1 Tbsp rosehip essential oil**
- ☐ **1 Tbsp pure aloe vera gel**
- ☐ **5 ml bottle with rollerball**

HOW TO MAKE IT

1 Combine the oils with the aloe vera gel in the bottle.

2 Shake well and apply under the eyes at night before going to bed or first thing in the morning.

3 Blend in with your finger. Avoid applying pressure as this can make eye puffiness worse.

4 Follow up with a cooling eye mask treatment.

Teas

For as long as humans have been able to warm water, they have enjoyed herbal teas. Herbal teas are not really true teas like green, black, and oolong tea, which are all brewed from the leaves of the Camellia sinensis plant. Herbal teas can be made from any part of a plant, including the roots, leaves, flowers, seeds, berries, or bark, and they can sometimes contain thousands of different compounds, each with its own distinctive healing capabilities. Many people use herbal teas to relieve mild to moderate ailments such as an upset stomach, sore throat, stuffy nose, insomnia, or coughing. Here are some of my favorite and powerfully effective herbal tea recipes.

Insomnia Busting Tea

If you are plagued with restless sleep or insomnia, this ginger and rosebud tea can help. Loaded with relaxing properties that help you wind down, it is a perfect, pre-bed sleepy time tea. Enjoy a cup about an hour before bedtime.

WHAT YOU NEED

- ☐ 1-inch piece of ginger root
- ☐ 6-8 dried rosebuds
- ☐ 1 Tbsp raw local honey
- ☐ Water

HOW TO MAKE IT

1 Peel the ginger root and cut it into slices.

2 Boil 2 cups of water on the stove in a pot or kettle.

3 Add the ginger and flowers. Allow it to simmer for 2 minutes.

4 Stir in the honey until it is dissolved.

5 Strain out the ginger and flowers, pour into a cup, and enjoy.

Note

This tea is also excellent with the addition of dried chamomile.

Garlic Antioxidant Tea

Although it may not sound like the most delicious drink, a cup of garlic tea is one of the best ways to start your day. It is loaded with vitamins A, B, and C, along with antioxidants, fiber, manganese, and sulfur.

WHAT YOU NEED

- ☐ 1 cup boiling water
- ☐ 2 cloves garlic, crushed
- ☐ 1 Tbsp fresh ginger root, minced
- ☐ 1 Tbsp local raw honey
- ☐ Juice of one lemon

HOW TO MAKE IT

1 Add water to a saucepan and bring to a boil.

2 Add the garlic and ginger to the boiling water, then reduce to a simmer.

3 Simmer for 5 minutes.

4 Remove garlic tea from the heat and allow it to steep for 10 minutes.

5 Strain liquid into a cup, then add the raw honey and lemon juice. Stir well and enjoy!

Minty Iced Refresher Tea

This refreshing beverage is the perfect summer refreshment and a great way to use mint, which grows quickly. There are so many types of mint; try them all in this tea to find the one you like best, or just use whatever you have growing in your garden.

WHAT YOU NEED

- ☐ **1 large handful of fresh mint leaves**
- ☐ **8 cups plus ½ cup filtered water**
- ☐ **½ cup coconut sugar**
- ☐ **½ vanilla bean**

HOW TO MAKE IT

1 Wash mint leaves and remove the stems, place them in a heat-proof bowl.

2 Boil 8 cups of water and pour over the mint. Let it steep for 15 minutes, then strain - reserve the mint leaves. Transfer the tea to a pitcher or a glass jar and refrigerate.

3 Combine strained mint leaves, sugar, vanilla bean, and ½ cup water in a saucepan and bring to a simmer. Cover and continue to simmer for 10 minutes, then strain.

4 Transfer liquid to a small jar and place in the refrigerator.

5 Fill glasses with ice and pour in the tea. Add 3 teaspoons (or desired amount) of mint syrup to each glass - stir and sip.

Parsley and Cinnamon Immunity Tea

Parsley is a potent source of vitamins A, C, K, and folic acid. Rather than utilizing parsley on your plate, incorporate it into this delicious cinnamon apple tea for an immunity boost.

WHAT YOU NEED

- ☐ 1 organic apple
- ☐ ¼ cup fresh organic parsley leaves
- ☐ ½ tsp organic cinnamon
- ☐ ½ tsp organic pumpkin pie spice
- ☐ Pinch of organic nutmeg
- ☐ 1 cup boiling water

HOW TO MAKE IT

1 Dice the apple and mash lightly with a fork into the bottom of a mug.

2 Add the rest of the dry ingredients on top.

3 Boil the water and pour it into the mug.

4 Allow it to sit for 5 minutes.

5 Straining is an option, but you can also allow the apple and herbs to remain in the bottom of the mug for a stronger flavor.

Infused Vinegars

Making your own herbal-infused vinegar is easy, and the combination of ingredients you can use is almost endless. All you need is vinegar and your choice of fresh or dried herbs, a container to store the mixture, and basic kitchen utensils.

The vinegar

A high-quality apple cider vinegar like Bragg's is recommended, as ACV offers extensive health benefits and can lower blood sugar and blood pressure, promote heart health, and encourage better digestion. Plus, it is an effective antimicrobial. If you plan to use it for cooking, a white wine or red wine vinegar can be used. Distilled white vinegar should never be used as it can be derived from petroleum and offers few health benefits.

Herbs

You can use just about any fresh or dried herbs or a combination of both. Keep in mind that dried herbs impart a stronger, deeper flavor, while fresh herbs provide a lighter, more delicate taste. Herbs that are especially nutrient-rich such as nettle, dandelion, red clover, and chickweed are all great choices. For culinary use, garlic, rosemary, oregano, thyme, hot peppers, tarragon, dill, and basil are popular options.

Vinegar flavored with garlic smells excellent, and it's a great herb to combine with others like basil, lemon balm, and thyme. To add it, just peel a clove and put it into your jar with your other herbs. If you've never made or even tasted an herbal-infused vinegar, you may want to start with a small batch by halving the recipe to fit a half-pint jar first. If it turns out well and you like it, you can make a full-sized batch the next time. Enjoy!

Basic Herbal Vinegar

You don't need much in the way of supplies or equipment, but it is essential to remember **never** to use reactive metal bowls, utensils, or containers, as vinegar will corrode active metals. Aluminum and copper are known to be the worst offenders. If you plan to store your vinegar in a Mason jar with a metal lid, you'll need to place a piece of wax paper over the mouth of the jar before capping it.

WHAT YOU NEED:

- ☐ **Vinegar**
- ☐ **Herbs**
- ☐ **Cutting board**
- ☐ **Knife**
- ☐ **Measuring cups**
- ☐ **Sterilized container with lid**
- ☐ **Bamboo skewer or wooden chopstick**
- ☐ **Wax paper, if needed**
- ☐ **Masking tape and pen**

Note

To strain and bottle, you'll need another sterilized container with a lid, a stainless steel or nylon mesh strainer, a glass bowl, a piece of muslin or cheesecloth, and a new label.

The ratio for ingredients can vary depending on what you're looking for, but it is generally 1 cup of dried herbs to 2 cups of vinegar. If you want something with more flavor or medicinal properties, use a little more of the herbs.

HOW TO DO IT

1 Sterilize your jars by using boiling water as you would for canning or running them through the dishwasher's wash and dry settings.

2 Add your herbs to the jar, followed by the vinegar. You may want to gently heat your vinegar before pouring it in to facilitate extraction. As dried herbs tend to float, you'll need your skewer or chopstick to submerge the herbs to get them completely soaked, so all trapped air bubbles are released.

3 Cap the jar, placing the wax paper over the mouth first if using a metal lid, and label it using masking tape and a marker. Be sure to include the name of the preparation, the ingredients, the date it was made, and the date it will be ready.

4 Store the jar in an area out of direct light.

5 If you've packed your jar full, check on it the day after it's made to be sure that the herbs are all submerged. If not, top off the jar with more vinegar and recap. Shake it every 2 to 3 days to help keep everything well mixed.

6 Allow the mixture to 'stew' for 2 to 4 weeks before straining and storing. For straining, use a clean piece of muslin fabric inside of a stainless steel mesh strainer. Be sure to squeeze or press out as much of the liquid as possible from the herbs.

Fire Cider

Fire cider is a medicinal concoction that has been used for many generations to support healthy digestion, keep away seasonal infections, boost circulation, and get rid of sinus congestion. It is essentially a collection of health-boosting herbs and vegetables, which are mixed together and soaked in vinegar over a period of time.

The vinegar draws out the active medicinal constituents of the plants and increases their nutrient potency. The recipe for fire cider will vary depending on the availability of the various ingredients and the maker's preferences. Some people choose to sweeten it with honey to take the edge off the heat and spice. Raw honey is a holistic medicinal food in itself!

Whichever blend you decide to use for your cider, the result will be antibacterial and antiviral. It will help provide potent antioxidants and warming spices to support robust immunity and digestion and makes a great addition to your toxin-free natural medicine cabinet.

WHAT YOU NEED

- ☐ ½ cup horseradish, peeled and diced
- ☐ ½ cup garlic, peeled and diced
- ☐ ½ cup, onion peeled and diced
- ☐ ¼ cup ginger, peeled and diced
- ☐ ¼ cup turmeric, peeled and diced

- ☐ 1 habanero chili, split in half
- ☐ 1 orange, quartered and thinly sliced crosswise
- ☐ ½ lemon, quartered and thinly sliced crosswise
- ☐ ½ cup parsley, chopped
- ☐ 2 Tbsp rosemary, chopped
- ☐ 2 Tbsp thyme, chopped
- ☐ 1 tsp black peppercorns
- ☐ 2 to 3 cups raw unfiltered apple cider vinegar (at least 5% acidity)
- ☐ ¼ cup raw honey, or more to taste

HOW TO MAKE IT

1 Place all of the vegetables, fruits, herbs, and spices in a clean 1-quart jar.

2 Fill the jar with vinegar, cover all the ingredients and make sure there are no air bubbles. Cap the jar. If using a metal lid, place a piece of parchment or wax paper between the jar and the lid to prevent corrosion. Shake well.

3 Let the jar sit for 4-6 weeks and shake daily.

4 Strain the vinegar into a clean jar and add honey to taste.

5 Refrigerate and use within a year.

Compresses, Poultices, and Plasters

Applying herbs to the skin can stop bleeding, reduce pain, stop itching and inflammation, encourage healing, stimulate organ function, and protect against infection. The skin is the body's largest organ and readily absorbs plant chemicals, taking them into the bloodstream and benefiting your internal system.

To make a compress, dip a soft, clean cloth into an herbal tea made with fresh or dried herbs. Apply the cloth to the affected area. Cold compresses can ease headaches, ease the pain of minor bumps and bruises, and reduce swelling. Hot compresses can relieve muscle pain and speed wound healing.

A poultice is similar to a compress, but it uses the fresh herbs instead of an herbal extract. To make a poultice, use dried herbs or herbal powders and hot water to create a paste. Additional ingredients may also be added, depending on what you are using the poultice for.

If you use fresh herbs, be sure to break them down to release their therapeutic properties. A blender works great, or you can crush them with a mallet or simply chew them up if you're in a pinch. Apply the paste directly on the skin and cover with gauze. Some herbs, such as ginger and comfrey, should be applied to a buffer cloth first as they can irritate sensitive skin. To keep poultices warm, place a hot water bottle or heating pad on top. For a cold poultice, use cold water or an ice pack.

Plasters are similar to poultices, but they use dried or powdered herbs mixed with a carrier such as clay, flour, ground flaxseed, or oatmeal to create a paste when mixed with hot water. Apply the hot paste to a clean piece of cotton cloth and place over the affected area. Cover this with another strip of cloth and use additional thin strips to hold the plaster in place and keep the heat in. Apply a thin layer of oil to protect the skin before using and always test the temperature of the plaster before applying.

Pain Reducing Cold Compress

When this cold compress is applied, it will reduce swelling and inflammation while combating minor to moderate pain. This is especially helpful when you want to reduce heat to the area since a cold compress will constrict blood vessels. It can help soothe rashes and other inflammatory skin conditions.

WHAT YOU NEED

- ☐ **Clean organic cotton cloth**
- ☐ **2 Tbsp fresh dill**
- ☐ **2 Tbsp fresh rosemary**
- ☐ **2 Tbsp dried lavender**

HOW TO MAKE IT

1 Make an herbal tea by steeping your herbs in hot water. Pour hot water directly onto your dill, lavender and rosemary. You can also create a little herbal pouch using a muslin bag or gauze.

2 Once you've made a potent blend, add it to a plastic container and place in the freezer until slushy.

3 Soak a clean cloth and apply the herbal compress to the affected area(s).

4 Leave on for 20 minutes. Apply this compress three times daily or until no longer needed.

Feel Better Fast Poultice

This poultice is the perfect combination when you are feeling under the weather. The ingredients in this poultice support the immune system, reduce inflammation, promote energy, and help with respiration.

WHAT YOU NEED

- ☐ 2 Tbsp turmeric, freshly grated or chopped
- ☐ 2 Tbsp lemongrass, chopped
- ☐ ½ cup raw onion, sliced
- ☐ 2 garlic cloves, chopped
- ☐ 2 Tbsp ginger, freshly grated or chopped
- ☐ 1 tsp coconut oil
- ☐ 2 drops oregano essential oil

- ☐ 10 drops eucalyptus
- ☐ White cloth, muslin, or a waterproof food wrap
- ☐ Thick string

HOW TO MAKE IT

1. Heat the coconut oil in a pan on low. Add the ginger, turmeric, lemongrass, onion, and garlic, and saute it for a few seconds. Turn the stove off and pour ingredients into a bowl. Let cool.

2. Add essential oils and stir.

3. Lay out the cloth, take a heaping tablespoon of the mixture, and place it in the center.

4. Fold the cloth to make a pack. Ensure that nothing falls out. Use a string if necessary to hold it together.

5. Place the poultice on your chest or other affected area for 20-30 minutes 2-3 times a day.

6. Place the poultice in the refrigerator and reheat in the microwave for up to 4 more uses.

Tinctures

Tinctures are concentrated herbal extracts that can be taken by themselves or added to syrups, salves, and lotions. All tinctures are extracts, but not all extracts are tinctures. Tinctures are a great way to preserve herbs and their medicinal properties for future use by infusing them in an alcohol base, while extracts can be made with any liquid and may not last as long.

Mood Lifting Tincture

If you are feeling a bit blue, this is the perfect mood-lifting tincture.

WHAT YOU NEED

- ☐ ¼ cup dried Saint John's wort flowers and leaves
- ☐ 1 tsp dried rose petals
- ☐ 1 tsp dried calendula flowers
- ☐ ¾ cup vodka
- ☐ Clean, pint-sized jar with lid
- ☐ Cheesecloth or fine mesh sieve
- ☐ Dark-colored dropper bottle

HOW TO MAKE IT

1 Mix the Saint John's wort, rose petals, calendula flowers and vodka in a half-pint jar and cover with a lid.

2 Store the jar in a cool, dark place for 4-6 weeks.

3 Strain out the herbs.

4 Store the tincture in a dropper bottle.

5 Take 1 teaspoon twice daily to enhance mood. Take for 2-3 weeks and then take one week off before starting again.

Cold and Flu Tincture

This antibacterial, antifungal, antiviral, and anti-inflammatory tincture will help you get over a cold, fight the flu, and reduce allergy symptoms.

WHAT YOU NEED

- ☐ ¼ cup dried echinacea
- ☐ ¾ cup vodka
- ☐ Glass jar with lid
- ☐ Cheesecloth or fine-mesh sieve
- ☐ Dark-colored dropper bottle

HOW TO MAKE IT

1 Place the dried echinacea in a clean jar.

2 Pour vodka into the jar, leaving 1 inch at the top.

3 Seal tightly and label jar.

4 Store the tincture for 4-6 weeks, shaking every now and then. Make sure to keep it at room temperature.

5 Strain the herbs out of the tincture and store in a dropper bottle.

6 Take 1/2 a teaspoon 3 times daily, as needed.

Calming Tincture

This tincture is the perfect remedy when you are feeling anxious and overwhelmed.

WHAT YOU NEED

- ☐ ¼ cup dried lavender flowers
- ☐ ¾ cup vodka
- ☐ Glass jar with lid
- ☐ Cheesecloth or fine-mesh sieve
- ☐ Dark-colored dropper bottle

HOW TO MAKE IT

1 Place dried flowers in a mason jar.

2 Pour vodka over flowers and seal.

3 Place the jar in a cool, dark place and label.

4 Store for 7 days, shaking occasionally.

5 Strain out flowers and take ½ a teaspoon orally as needed.

Balms and Creams

Topical remedies containing herbs nourish your skin and create a natural shield that helps protect the skin and facilitate nutrient absorption. Infused oils are made by steeping dried herbs in a carrier oil such as almond or olive to extract the therapeutic compounds. Once they are infused with herbs, these beneficial oils can keep for up to one year and can be used for salves and creams, among other things. Balms are a combination of infused oil and wax such as soy or beeswax, while lotions and creams are a lighter texture and are made by combining the oil with water.

Headache Relief Rosemary Balm

When the tension of a hard day turns into a headache,
this rosemary balm offers relief.

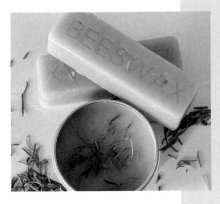

WHAT YOU NEED

- ☐ **2 sprigs fresh rosemary**
- ☐ **1 part organic coconut oil**
- ☐ **1 part organic shea butter**
- ☐ **1 part local,
  organic beeswax**
- ☐ **5 drops rosemary
  essential oil**
- ☐ **5 drops lavender
  essential oil**
- ☐ **Lip balm containers
  or small jars**

HOW TO MAKE IT

1 Set up a double boiler, combine coconut oil and rosemary leaves on low heat.

2 Simmer on low for 2 hours, then strain into a jar.

3 Add the rosemary-infused oil along with the shea butter and beeswax to your double boiler.

4 Once melted, remove from heat and add the essential oils.

5 Pour into the jar of your choice. Lip balm containers work well for a quick application on the go, allowing you to rub your temples or any other affected area with ease.

Lemongrass and Peppermint Energizing Balm

This balm contains two oils that will invigorate and energize while chasing stress out the door. It is easy to make and can be used anywhere on your skin. Just rub some on and feel your stress start to melt away.

WHAT YOU NEED

- ☐ **3 Tbsp coconut oil**
- ☐ **3 Tbsp beeswax**
- ☐ **1 Tbsp shea butter**
- ☐ **2 Tbsp almond oil**
- ☐ **45 drops peppermint essential oil**
- ☐ **30 drops lemongrass essential oil**
- ☐ **Metal tins or any other containers of your choice**

HOW TO MAKE IT

1 Measure out the coconut oil, beeswax, and shea butter and place in a glass microwavable measuring cup.

2 Heat slowly in the microwave in 30-second intervals until completely melted.

3 Add the almond oil and stir well. Let the mixture cool on the counter for a few minutes before adding the essential oils.

4 Add the essential oils and quickly pour into your containers.

5 Allow the mixture to set up completely. Place containers in the refrigerator to speed up the hardening process.

6 Use as much and as often as you like.

Soothing Orange Lip Butter

Apply this soothing lip balm to dry, chapped, or sunburned lips.

WHAT YOU NEED

☐ **1 Tbsp organic shea butter**

☐ **3 Tbsp calendula herbal oil**

☐ **1 Tbsp plus 1 tsp beeswax**

☐ **10-15 drops sweet orange essential oil**

☐ **A few drops organic vitamin E oil**

☐ **Lip balm tubes or small containers**

WHAT TO DO:

1 Coarsely chop the beeswax and place beeswax, shea butter, and oil in a small pot or glass measuring cup.

2 Gently heat in the top of a double boiler until the beeswax and butter have melted.

3 Remove from the stovetop and stir in the essential oil and vitamin E oil.

4 Quickly pour the mixture into lip balm tubes or small containers.

5 This recipe should make approximately 1.5 oz of lip balm, enough to fill 10 lip balm tubes.

Burn Ease

There is no arguing that honey - especially Manuka honey - is loaded with medicinal properties. It is antibacterial and anti-inflammatory and can promote the healing of minor burns even better than over-the-counter antibiotic cream. Lavender contains pain-relieving and antimicrobial properties and can reduce inflammation and speed wound recovery while adding a delightful scent that can help ease stress and anxiety. Chamomile is very soothing to the skin and will reduce swelling and redness. Keep a tin of this in your kitchen for minor burns.

WHAT YOU NEED

- ¼ cup calendula infused oil
- 1 heaping tsp beeswax pellets
- ¼ cup Manuka honey
- 1 tsp vitamin E oil
- 20 drops lavender essential oil
- 10 drops chamomile essential oil
- Clean, discarded tin can
- 2-ounce metal tins

HOW TO MAKE IT

1 Wash and dry discarded tin can. Add oil and beeswax and place it inside a pot filled with 1 inch of water.

2 Bring the water to a simmer over low heat so that the oil and beeswax melt. When melted, remove from the heat.

3 Add the lavender and chamomile oils and the vitamin E oil and stir well.

4 Pour mixture into metal tins and let cool for about 8 hours. Place the cap on the tins and store in a cool, dark place for up to a year.

5 Use on minor burns after first running burn area under cool water and patting dry. Apply the balm liberally to the affected area and cover with a clean piece of gauze dressing or leave it exposed to the air. Reapply as needed to ease pain, swelling, and encourage healing.

Steams

Not only does an herbal steam make your home smell great, but it is also rich in therapeutic benefits. One example is an herbal steam made with peppermint and eucalyptus to help with congestion and ease breathing. I can remember placing herbs such as thyme, rosemary, and oregano in a bowl of hot water and creating a "breathing treatment" for my kids when they were younger and suffering from a cold. They willingly took their position under the towel and gently breathed in the herbal goodness. Steams are also great for the skin, opening up pores and pulling out toxins.

Wellness Steam

This steam is loaded with herbs that help open up your airway, break down mucus and help eliminate cold symptoms. Repeat as necessary until you feel better. This steam is also the perfect option for opening up pores, improving circulation, and softening your skin. **Note:** All herbs are dry.

WHAT YOU NEED

- ☐ 1 Tbsp thyme
- ☐ 1 Tbsp rosemary
- ☐ 1 Tbsp basil
- ☐ 1 Tbsp peppermint leaf
- ☐ 1 Tbsp eucalyptus
- ☐ 1 Tbsp lavender flowers
- ☐ Juice from one lemon
- ☐ Glass bowl with a lid
- ☐ Hot water
- ☐ Towel

HOW TO MAKE IT

1 Place a large glass bowl on your kitchen table on a hot pad or towel.

2 Boil water in a tea kettle and pour about 2 inches into the bowl.

3 Add the herbs and lemon juice and cover the bowl with the lid for 2 minutes.

4 Remove the lid and check the temperature to ensure it is not too hot for your face.

5 Lower your head, so that it is comfortably above the bowl and steam and then cover your head with a towel.

6 Slowly breathe in the steam through your nose and out through your mouth for 10 minutes.

7 When finished, pour out the water and herbs and wash the bowl thoroughly.

8 Wipe your face with a mixture of 1 part apple cider vinegar and 1 part water to tone skin and remove any debris from loosened pores.

Note

Use as many or as few herbs as you like. For further benefit for congestion, add 5 drops of eucalyptus essential oil to the mixture.

Infused Oils

An infused herbal oil is crafted by using a fixed oil such as jojoba, olive, fractionated (MCT) coconut, or sunflower and combining it with fresh or dried plant material and leaving it to steep for several weeks. This softens the plant material and allows the essential oils to mix with the carrier oil, which produces an infused aromatic oil that can be used in baths, in herbal preparations, in culinary creations, or topically.

Note

Both dry and fresh herbs and flowers can be used as long as fresh plant material is permitted to wilt for at least 12 hours to remove moisture.

Calendula Infused Oil

This oil can be used in cooking, dressings, marinades, applied topically as a massage oil, or used in other herbal healing preparations.

WHAT YOU NEED

- ☐ **Organic olive oil**
- ☐ **Organic calendula flowers**

HOW TO MAKE IT

1 Place calendula flowers in a clean, dry glass jar. Wilt fresh calendula for 12 hours to remove the moisture before adding it to the jar.

2 Pour olive oil into the jar, making sure to cover the flowers by at least 1 inch of oil, so they have space to expand. Stir well and cap the jar tightly.

3 Let the jar sit on a warm, sunny windowsill and shake gently at least once daily.

4 After 4-6 weeks, strain the herbs out, pour the infused oil into glass bottles, and store in a cool, dark place.

Sun Infused Herbal Oil

Oils infused using this solar method are great for body care recipes as well as culinary recipes.

WHAT YOU NEED

☐ Clean, quart-size jar with lid
☐ Dry or fresh herbs
☐ Carrier oil such as extra virgin olive oil
☐ Label

HOW TO MAKE IT

1 Place herbs in the jar, leaving about 3 inches of open space.

2 Fill the jar with oil and make sure that herbs are covered by at least an inch.

3 If any herbs sneak to the surface during the infusion process, pour in more oil. If any herb pieces float to the top and begin to mold or decay, skim them off.

4 Cap the jar tightly and shake. Place in a sunny, warm windowsill and shake three times a day.

5 After 3 weeks, strain the herbs using a cheesecloth and be sure to squeeze out as much oil as possible. Pour the oil into clean glass bottles, label, and date.

6 Oils will keep for up to a year when stored in a cool, dark place. If you are using the oil topically, add a tablespoon of vitamin E oil. This will help prolong the shelf life and benefit your skin.

Cayenne Pepper Joint Remedy

Several studies have shown that the capsaicin in cayenne pepper can reduce pain and improve impaired mobility associated with rheumatoid arthritis and osteoarthritis. This cayenne pepper remedy employs the substance P-blocking power of capsaicin to provide immediate, side-effect-free relief from joint pain.

WHAT YOU NEED

☐ **3 medium dried cayenne peppers**

☐ **2 cups olive oil**

☐ **Double boiler**

☐ **Water**

☐ **Strainer**

HOW TO MAKE IT

1 Roughly chop up the cayenne peppers and place them on the top of a double boiler.

2 Pour in around two cups of extra virgin olive oil, fill the bottom of the double boiler with water, and place it over low heat.

3 Leave the cayenne and olive oil simmering on low for 2 ½ hours, then remove from heat.

4 Allow the mixture to cool to room temperature, then pour it through a fine-mesh strainer into a glass bottle or jar.

5 Store in a dark cupboard, and massage a small amount of the oil into sore or stiff joints two to three times per day.

Compound Butters

Herb butter, also known as compound butter, is butter that is mixed with fresh or dried herbs. It is usually formed into a log, chilled, and sliced for serving. Herb butters are a delicious way to use your herbs and enjoy bold flavors and beautiful color. You can use salted or unsalted butter. Compound butter is *so* simple yet delicious and impressive. I love to make compound butter with mint, tarragon, basil, chives, and parsley, as well as rosemary and sage.

Rosemary and Sage Butter

When going to a dinner party or a holiday meal, this is an excellent quick and easy gift that you can wrap with care. Don't be afraid to get creative! Add any spices, herbs, or other flavorful ingredients that you want to your recipe. You can even add edible flowers for additional color.

WHAT YOU NEED

- ☐ 1 cup — or 2 sticks of organic, grass-fed butter (softened)
- ☐ 1 Tbsp sage, chopped
- ☐ ½ Tbsp rosemary, chopped
- ☐ 2 Tbsp fennel seeds
- ☐ Wax paper
- ☐ Wooden spoon

HOW TO MAKE IT

1 Toast the fennel seeds on low heat, adding your chopped sage and rosemary for the last minute or so.

2 Remove from heat, allow to cool, and pour into a bowl with butter.

3 Using a mixer or wooden spoon, incorporate the sage, rosemary, and fennel seeds so that they're evenly distributed.

4 Place this combination on a piece of wax paper, rolling tight so that you make a "log."

5 Twist both ends so that the combination is tightly closed.

6 Store in the fridge for 2 hours before cutting slices.

Infused Honey

Herbal infused honey is not only a flavorful way to reap all the therapeutic benefits of honey and herbs but it is also a versatile complement to many culinary creations. Dried herbal leaf and flower material, along with local raw honey, work best, and the options for creating herbal infused honey are endless. Here are some of my favorite herbs to use.

- Lavender
- Lemon Balm
- Basil
- Chamomile
- Sage
- Thyme
- Ginger
- Peppermint
- Rosemary

Basic Infused Honey

WHAT YOU NEED

- ☐ Dried herbs and spices
- ☐ Raw, local honey
- ☐ Glass quart jar with tight-fitting lid
- ☐ Chopstick

HOW TO MAKE IT

1 Fill the jar just under half full with herbs and spices.

2 Pour honey into the jar and make sure all herbs are submerged. Use the chopstick to push the herbs down.

3 Place a lid on the jar and put it in a sunny windowsill. It needs to be kept warm for proper infusion.

4 Turn the jar over once per day. Add more honey if needed to keep herbs covered.

5 Allow the mixture to infuse for 2-4 weeks. A longer infusion time means a stronger flavor.

6 Strain out the herbs and keep them to add to teas and warm drinks.

7 Store infused honey in a cool, dark place in a tightly sealed jar to maintain freshness.

Sore Throat Soothing Honey

Ease a sore throat and cough with this tasty herbal remedy
guaranteed to help you feel better.

WHAT YOU NEED

- ¼ cup fresh sage leaves
- ½ cup fresh oregano leaves
- ½ cup fresh sliced ginger
- 1 cup raw local honey

HOW TO MAKE IT

1. Place sage, oregano, and ginger in a sealable jar.

2. Pour honey over leaves and stir to mix well.

3. Let the mixture sit for 1 week, stirring daily.

4. Strain out leaves. Take 1 teaspoon as needed to ease a sore
   throat.

Infused Salts and Sugars

One of my favorite ways to preserve and enjoy all the benefits
of herbs is to infuse them in salts and sugars. Although I rarely
use added sugar or salt, adding my favorite herbs makes a treat
that I can use in special drinks, baked goods, or even in personal
care products. In addition, infused salt and sugars make a great
homemade gift to share with others. It takes about a week to infuse
salt and sugar fully, but the resulting product will keep for up to 3
months.

Thyme and Oregano Salt

This salt is delicious paired with garlic bread, watermelon, tomatoes, potatoes, pasta or even corn the cob

WHAT YOU NEED

- ☐ ⅓ cup packed, fresh basil and thyme mixed
- ☐ 1 cup coarse sea salt or rock salt
- ☐ Blender

HOW TO MAKE IT

1   Preheat the oven to 220 degrees F.

2   Chop fresh herbs, stems and leaves, into small pieces and add to the blender.

3   Add salt to the blender and pulse for two minutes until basil is broken up and mixed with the salt. You may have to push the mixture together with a rubber spatula as it can get stuck in the bottom of the blender.

4   Spread the salt mixture on a large baking sheet and bake for 30 minutes until the salt is dry - stir partway through.

5   The salt will be a lighter shade of green once dry.

6   Break apart clumps with a wooden spoon and transfer salt to small glass jars.

Pineapple Mint Sugar

Use this delicious pineapple mint sugar in your favorite teas or other beverages and baked goods. You can also add a little coconut oil to make a sugar foot scrub.

WHAT YOU NEED

- ☐ **Fresh pineapple mint leaves**
- ☐ **1 cup coconut sugar**
- ☐ **Container with lid**

HOW TO MAKE IT

1 Rinse pineapple mint leaves and pat them dry.

2 Place a layer of pineapple mint leaves in the bottom of a jar or container with a lid.

3 Add a ¼-inch layer of sugar on top.

4 Repeat this layering process until the jar is full, ending with a sugar layer.

5 Seal the jar and put it in a cool, dark place for 2 weeks before using.

6 Sugar will keep in a pantry for up to a year.

Pamper Yourself

Herbs are soothing, cooling, refreshing, and excellent additions to your self-care routine. Make time for yourself weekly to relax and unwind with the help of these easy-to-make herbal preparations.

Thyme Soothing Bath Soak

WHAT YOU NEED

- ☐ 1 cup Epsom salt
- ☐ 1 handful fresh thyme
- ☐ 10 drops thyme essential oil
- ☐ 1 tsp olive oil (optional)

HOW TO MAKE IT

1 Simply combine all ingredients and pour them into a hot bath.

2 Soak in this remedy once daily until your symptoms subside.

Oatmeal Herb Face Scrub

This is the perfect weekly scrub to remove dead skin cells and kick up circulation. It has a mild exfoliating action that will leave your skin feeling baby soft and radiant.

WHAT YOU NEED

- ☐ 1 cup rolled oats
- ☐ ⅓ cup cornmeal
- ☐ ⅓ cup lavender, peppermint, and calendula, dried
- ☐ 1 Tbsp sugar

HOW TO MAKE IT

1 Mix the oatmeal, cornmeal, herbs, and sugar in a clean coffee grinder and grind into a fine powder.

2 Store in a sealed container in a dry, cool location for up to 3 months.

3 When ready to use, put a little mixture in the palm of your hand and add enough warm water to create a paste. Massage gently into clean skin, using your fingertips in a circular motion.

4 Rinse, pat dry, and follow up with your favorite organic moisturizer.

Tired Tootsies Foot Soak

This herbal foot soak is the perfect way to end a long day on your feet. Pamper your tootsies with the combination of healing and cooling essential oils and herbs.

WHAT YOU NEED

- ☐ **2 cups Epsom salt**
- ☐ **8 drops lavender essential oil**
- ☐ **6 drops mint essential oil**
- ☐ **2 drops eucalyptus essential oil**
- ☐ **2 drops rosemary essential oil**
- ☐ **1 tsp dried comfrey root powder**
- ☐ **1 tsp dried lavender**
- ☐ **1 tsp wild bergamot**
- ☐ **Dried orange slices**
- ☐ **1 tsp dried mint leaves**

HOW TO MAKE IT

1 Fill a glass jar halfway with Epsom salt.

2 Add the essential oils, put the lid on and shake.

3 Remove the lid, add the dried herbs and dried orange slices and shake again.

4 To use, add ¼ cup to a warm foot bath and soak for 15 minutes.

The Green Gift That Keeps On Giving

Whether you share collected seeds, cuttings, divisions, homemade elixirs, tonics, vinegar, salves, teas, or other herbal preparations, plants keep giving and giving. In this book, I have just grazed the tip of the wide world of medicinal plants, but I hope that this has invigorated your sense of what is achievable and motivated you to keep learning, planting, and sharing.

Humanity's first and most powerful pharmacy was found in nature. Today modern medicine still relies on natural compounds for medical advancement and the formulation of new drugs. Through trial and error, our ancestors discovered the power behind the pretty plants that decorate the landscape. This knowledge has been passed down and added to throughout countless generations and cultures spanning the entire globe.

Never underestimate the power of plants, but instead learn to respect, value, and use them for good!

Happy Growing!

Sources

Aloe

C;, Maenthaisong R;Chaiyakunapruk N;Niruntraporn S;Kongkaew. "The Efficacy of Aloe Vera Used for Burn Wound Healing: a Systematic Review." *Burns : Journal of the International Society for Burn Injuries*, U.S. National Library of Medicine, 2007, pubmed. ncbi.nlm.nih.gov/17499928/.

Radha, Maharjan H., and Nampoothiri P. Laxmipriya. "Evaluation of Biological Properties and Clinical Effectiveness of Aloe Vera: A Systematic Review." *Journal of Traditional and Complementary Medicine*, Elsevier, 23 Dec. 2014, www.sciencedirect.com/science/article/pii/S2225411014000078.

S;, Somboonwong J;Thanamittramanee S;Jariyapongskul A;Patumraj. "Therapeutic Effects of Aloe Vera on Cutaneous Microcirculation and Wound Healing in Second Degree Burn Model in Rats." *Journal of the Medical Association of Thailand = Chotmaihet Thangphaet*, U.S. National Library of Medicine, 2000, pubmed.ncbi.nlm.nih.gov/10808702/.

Surjushe, Amar, et al. "Aloe Vera: a Short Review." *Indian Journal of Dermatology*, Medknow Publications, 2008, www.ncbi.nlm.nih.gov/pmc/articles/PMC2763764/.

Anise

D;, Kosalec I;Pepeljnjak S;Kustrak. "Antifungal Activity of Fluid Extract and Essential Oil from Anise Fruits (Pimpinella Anisum L., Apiaceae)." Acta Pharmaceutica (Zagreb, Croatia), U.S. National Library of Medicine, 2005, pubmed.ncbi.nlm.nih.gov/16375827/.

Shahamat, Zahra, et al. "Evaluation of Antidepressant-like Effects of Aqueous and Ethanolic Extracts of Pimpinella Anisum Fruit in Mice." Avicenna Journal of Phytomedicine, Mashhad University of Medical Sciences, 2016, www.ncbi.nlm.nih.gov/pmc/articles/PMC4930539/.

Tabanca N;Khan SI;Bedir E;Annavarapu S;Willett K;Khan IA;Kirimer N;Baser KH; "Estrogenic Activity of Isolated Compounds and Essential Oils of Pimpinella Species from Turkey, Evaluated Using a Recombinant Yeast Screen." Planta Medica, U.S. National Library of Medicine, 2004, pubmed.ncbi.nlm.nih.gov/15368661/.

Basil

·················

Ali SS;Abd El Wahab MG;Ayuob NN;Suliaman M; "The Antidepressant-like Effect of Ocimum Basilicum in an Animal Model of Depression." Biotechnic & Histochemistry : Official Publication of the Biological Stain Commission, U.S. National Library of Medicine, 2017, pubmed.ncbi.nlm.nih.gov/28800278/.

Cohen, Marc Maurice. "Tulsi - Ocimum Sanctum: A Herb for All Reasons." Journal of Ayurveda and Integrative Medicine, Medknow Publications & Media Pvt Ltd, 2014, www.ncbi.nlm.nih.gov/pmc/articles/PMC4296439/.

J;, Varney E;Buckle. "Effect of Inhaled Essential Oils on Mental Exhaustion and Moderate Burnout: a Small Pilot Study." Journal of Alternative and Complementary Medicine (New York, N.Y.), U.S. National Library of Medicine, 2013, pubmed.ncbi.nlm.nih.gov/23140115/.

Rasul, A, and N Akhtar. "Formulation and in Vivo Evaluation for Anti-Aging Effects of an Emulsion Containing Basil Extract Using Non- Invasive Biophysical Techniques." Daru : Journal of Faculty of Pharmacy, Tehran University of Medical Sciences, Tehran University of Medical Sciences, 2011, www.ncbi.nlm.nih.gov/pmc/articles/PMC3304398/.

Widjaja, Sry Suryani, et al. "Glucose Lowering Effect of Basil Leaves in Diabetic Rats." Open Access Macedonian Journal of Medical Sciences, Republic of Macedonia, 5 May 2019, www.ncbi.nlm.nih.gov/pmc/articles/PMC6542390/.

Bee Balm

···························

"Chemical Composition, Antifungal and In Vitro Antioxidant Properties of Monarda Didyma L. Essential Oil." *Taylor & Francis*, 2011, www.tandfonline.com/doi/abs/10.1080/10412905.2006.9699174.

Johnson, Posted ByJackie. "Benefits of Bee Balm: Monarda Fistulosa and M. Didyma." *Herbal Academy*, 25 Jan. 2018, theherbalacademy.com/benefits-of-bee-balm-monarda-fistulosa-and-m-didyma/.

Lu, Zhan Guo, et al. "Chemical Composition of Antibacterial Activity of Essential Oil from Monarda Citriodora Flowers." *Advanced Materials Research*, Trans Tech Publications Ltd, 20 Jan. 2011, www.scientific.net/AMR.183-185.920.

Broadleaf Plantain

Hussan, Farida, et al. "Anti-Inflammatory Property of Plantago Major Leaf Extract Reduces the Inflammatory Reaction in Experimental Acetaminophen-Induced Liver Injury." *Evidence-Based Complementary and Alternative Medicine : ECAM*, Hindawi Publishing Corporation, 2015, www.ncbi.nlm.nih.gov/pmc/articles/PMC4537734/.

Kurt B;Bilge N;Sözmen M;Aydın U;Önyay T;Özaydın I; "Effects of Plantago Lanceolata L. Extract on Full-Thickness Excisional Wound Healing in a Mouse Model." *Biotechnic & Histochemistry : Official Publication of the Biological Stain Commission*, U.S. National Library of Medicine, 2018, pubmed.ncbi.nlm.nih.gov/29575942/.

Najafian, Younes, et al. "Plantago Major in Traditional Persian Medicine and Modern Phytotherapy: a Narrative Review." *Electronic Physician*, Electronic Physician, 25 Feb. 2018, www.ncbi.nlm.nih.gov/pmc/articles/PMC5878035/.

Calendula

Duran V;Matic M;Jovanović M;Mimica N;Gajinov Z;Poljacki M;Boza P; "Results of the Clinical Examination of an Ointment with Marigold (Calendula Officinalis) Extract in the Treatment of Venous Leg Ulcers." *International Journal of Tissue Reactions*, U.S. National Library of Medicine, 2005, pubmed.ncbi.nlm.nih.gov/16372475/.

Fronza M;Heinzmann B;Hamburger M;Laufer S;Merfort I; "Determination of the Wound Healing Effect of Calendula Extracts Using the Scratch Assay with 3T3 Fibroblasts." *Journal of Ethnopharmacology*, U.S. National Library of Medicine, 2009, pubmed.ncbi.nlm.nih.gov/19781615/.

Panahi Y;Sharif MR;Sharif A;Beiraghdar F;Zahiri Z;Amirchoopani G;Marzony ET;Sahebkar A; "A Randomized Comparative Trial on the Therapeutic Efficacy of Topical Aloe Vera and Calendula Officinalis on Diaper Dermatitis in Children." *TheScientificWorldJournal*, U.S. National Library of Medicine, 2012, pubmed.ncbi.nlm.nih.gov/22606064/.

Catnip

Bol, Sebastiaan, et al. "Responsiveness of Cats (Felidae) to Silver Vine (Actinidia Polygama), Tatarian Honeysuckle (Lonicera Tatarica), Valerian (Valeriana Officinalis) and Catnip (Nepeta Cataria)." *BMC Veterinary Research*, BioMed Central, 16 Mar. 2017, bmcvetres.biomedcentral.com/articles/10.1186/s12917-017-0987-6.

Grognet, Jeff. "Catnip. Its Uses and Effects, Past and Present." *ncbi.nlm.nih.gov/pmc/articles/PMC1480656/pdf/canvetj00079-0049.pdf.*

McElvain,, S M, et al. "The Constituents of the Volatile Oil of Catnip. I. Nepetalic Acid, Nepetalactone and Related Compounds." *ACS Publications*, Journal of American Chemical Society , 1941.

Cayenne

Ludy, Mary-Jon, and Richard D. Mattes. "The Effects of Hedonically Acceptable Red Pepper Doses on Thermogenesis and Appetite." *Physiology & Behavior*, Elsevier, 18 Nov. 2010, www.sciencedirect.com/science/article/abs/pii/S0031938410004063.

Maji, Amal K, and Pratim Banerji. "Phytochemistry and Gastrointestinal Benefits of the Medicinal Spice, Capsicum Annuum L. (Chilli): a Review." *Journal of Complementary & Integrative Medicine*, U.S. National Library of Medicine, 2016, pubmed.ncbi.nlm.nih.gov/26756096/.

Surh, YJ. "More than Spice: Capsaicin in Hot Chili Peppers Makes Tumor Cells Commit Suicide." *Journal of the National Cancer Institute*, U.S. National Library of Medicine, 2002, pubmed.ncbi.nlm.nih.gov/12208886/.

Yang D;Luo Z;Ma S;Wong WT;Ma L;Zhong J;He H;Zhao Z;Cao T;Yan Z;Liu D;Arendshorst WJ;Huang Y;Tepel M;Zhu Z; "Activation of TRPV1 by Dietary Capsaicin Improves Endothelium-Dependent Vasorelaxation and Prevents Hypertension." *Cell Metabolism*, U.S. National Library of Medicine, 2010, pubmed.ncbi.nlm.nih. gov/20674858/.

Chamomile

College of Nursing and Health Professions. "Chamomile: A Spoonful of Medicine : Holistic Nursing Practice." *LWW*, 2008, journals.lww.com/hnpjournal/ Citation/2008/01000/Chamomile__A_Spoonful_of_Medicine.10.aspx.

Srivastava, Janmejai K, et al. "Chamomile: A Herbal Medicine of the Past with Bright Future." *Molecular Medicine Reports*, U.S. National Library of Medicine, 1 Nov. 2010, www. ncbi.nlm.nih.gov/pmc/articles/PMC2995283/.

Zadeth, Jalal B, et al. *Chamomile (Matricaria Recutita) As a Valuable Medicinal Plant*. International Journal of Advanced Biological and Biomedical Research, 2014, citeseerx.ist. psu.edu/viewdoc/download?doi=10.1.1.971.5120&rep=rep1&type=pdf.

Chickweed

Chandra, Satish, and D S Rawat. "Medicinal Plants of the Family Caryophyllaceae: a Review of Ethno-Medicinal Uses and Pharmacological Properties." *Integrative Medicine Research*, Elsevier, Sept. 2015, www.ncbi.nlm.nih.gov/pmc/articles/PMC5481791/.

Polito, Letizia, et al. "Plants Producing Ribosome-Inactivating Proteins in Traditional Medicine." *Molecules (Basel, Switzerland)*, MDPI, 18 Nov. 2016, www.ncbi.nlm.nih.gov/ pmc/articles/PMC6273415/.

Rani, Neerja, et al. "Quality Assessment and Anti-Obesity Activity of Stellaria Media (Linn.) Vill." *BMC Complementary and Alternative Medicine*, BioMed Central, 3 Sept. 2012, www.ncbi.nlm.nih.gov/pmc/articles/PMC3468403/.

Chives

Eisenhauer, Bronwyn, et al. "Lutein and Zeaxanthin-Food Sources, Bioavailability and Dietary Variety in Age-Related Macular Degeneration Protection." *Nutrients*, MDPI, 9 Feb. 2017, www.ncbi.nlm.nih.gov/pmc/articles/PMC5331551/.

Nicastro, Holly L., et al. "Garlic and Onions: Their Cancer Prevention Properties." *Cancer Prevention Research*, American Association for Cancer Research, 1 Mar. 2015, cancerpreventionresearch.aacrjournals.org/content/8/3/181.

Rattanachaikunsopon, P., and P. Phumkhachorn. "[PDF] Diallyl Sulfide Content and Antimicrobial Activity against Food-Borne Pathogenic Bacteria of Chives (Allium Schoenoprasum): Semantic Scholar." *Undefined*, 1 Jan. 1970, www.semanticscholar.org/paper/Diallyl-Sulfide-Content-and-Antimicrobial-Activity-Rattanachaikunsopon-Phumkhachorn/d642dd1ae41cc445751f19fecde3936952a00be2?p2df.

Seki, T., et al. "[PDF] Anticancer Effects of Diallyl Trisulfide Derived from Garlic.: Semantic Scholar." *Undefined*, 1 Jan. 1970, www.semanticscholar.org/paper/Anticancer-effects-of-diallyl-trisulfide-derived-Seki-Hosono/0e4e9ee430880233143d6db5f1a438c89299b569?p2df.

Štajner, D., et al. "Allium Schoenoprasum L., as a Natural Antioxidant." *Wiley Online Library*, John Wiley & Sons, Ltd, 3 Aug. 2004, onlinelibrary.wiley.com/doi/abs/10.1002/ptr.1472.

Chrysanthemum

Baek, Jong Min, et al. "Dual Effect of Chrysanthemum Indicum Extract to Stimulate Osteoblast Differentiation and Inhibit Osteoclast Formation and Resorption In Vitro." *Evidence-Based Complementary and Alternative Medicine*, Hindawi, 28 Oct. 2014, www.hindawi.com/journals/ecam/2014/176049/.

Luyen BT;Tai BH;Thao NP;Cha JY;Lee HY;Lee YM;Kim YH; "Anti-Inflammatory Components of Chrysanthemum Indicum Flowers." *Bioorganic & Medicinal Chemistry Letters*, U.S. National Library of Medicine, 2015, pubmed.ncbi.nlm.nih.gov/25497988/.

Shahrajabian, M Hesam, et al. "A REVIEW OF CHRYSANTHEMUM, THE EASTERN QUEEN IN TRADITIONAL CHINESE MEDICINE WITH HEALING POWER IN MODERN PHARMACEUTICAL SCIENCES." *Research Gate*, Applied Ecology and Environmental Research, 2019, www.researchgate.net/publication/336316194_A_REVIEW_OF_CHRYSANTHEMUM_THE_EASTERN_QUEEN_IN_TRADITIONAL_CHINESE_MEDICINE_WITH_HEALING_POWER_IN_MODERN_PHARMACEUTICAL_SCIENCES.

Cilantro

S;, Mahendra P;Bisht. "Anti-Anxiety Activity of Coriandrum Sativum Assessed Using Different Experimental Anxiety Models." *Indian Journal of Pharmacology*, U.S. National Library of Medicine, 2011, pubmed.ncbi.nlm.nih.gov/22022003/.

Smith, Gabriella E., et al. "If I Fits I Sits: A Citizen Science Investigation into Illusory Contour Susceptibility in Domestic Cats (Felis Silvestris Catus)." *Applied Animal Behaviour Science*, Elsevier, 30 Apr. 2021, www.sciencedirect.com/science/article/abs/pii/S0168159121001258.

Comfrey

Koll, R., et al. "Efficacy and Tolerance of a Comfrey Root Extract (Extr. Rad. Symphyti) in the Treatment of Ankle Distorsions: Results of a Multicenter, Randomized, Placebo-Controlled, Double-Blind Study." *Phytomedicine*, Urban & Fischer, 2 Sept. 2004, www.sciencedirect.com/science/article/abs/pii/S0944711304000327.

Staiger, Christiane. "Comfrey: a Clinical Overview." *Phytotherapy Research : PTR*, Blackwell Publishing Ltd, Oct. 2012, www.ncbi.nlm.nih.gov/pmc/articles/PMC3491633/.

Staiger, Christiane. "Comfrey Root: from Tradition to Modern Clinical Trials." *Wiener Medizinische Wochenschrift (1946)*, Springer Vienna, Feb. 2013, www.ncbi.nlm.nih.gov/pmc/articles/PMC3580139/.

Dandelion

Davaatseren, Munkhtugs, et al. "Taraxacum Official (Dandelion) Leaf Extract Alleviates High-Fat Diet-Induced Nonalcoholic Fatty Liver." *Food and Chemical Toxicology : an International Journal Published for the British Industrial Biological Research Association*, U.S. National Library of Medicine, 2013, pubmed.ncbi.nlm.nih.gov/23603008/.

Wirngo, Fonyuy E, et al. "The Physiological Effects of Dandelion (Taraxacum Officinale) in Type 2 Diabetes." *The Review of Diabetic Studies : RDS*, SBDR - Society for Biomedical Diabetes Research, 2016, www.ncbi.nlm.nih.gov/pmc/articles/PMC5553762/.

Dill

Goodarzi, Mohammad Taghi, et al. "The Role of Anethum Graveolens L. (Dill) in the Management of Diabetes." *NCBI*, Journal of Tropical Medicine, 2016, www.ncbi.nlm.nih.gov/pmc/articles/PMC5088306/.

Huang, Zhiyi, et al. "Role of Vitamin A in the Immune System." *Journal of Clinical Medicine*, MDPI, 6 Sept. 2018, www.ncbi.nlm.nih.gov/pmc/articles/PMC6162863/.

Pham-Huy, Lein Ai, et al. "Free Radicals, Antioxidants in Disease and Health." *NCBI*, International Journal of Biomedical Science, 2008, www.ncbi.nlm.nih.gov/pmc/articles/PMC3614697/.

S;, Carr AC;Maggini. "Vitamin C and Immune Function." *Nutrients*, U.S. National Library of Medicine, 2017, pubmed.ncbi.nlm.nih.gov/29099763/.

Echinacea

Chicca A;Adinolfi B;Martinotti E;Fogli S;Breschi MC;Pellati F;Benvenuti S;Nieri P; "Cytotoxic Effects of Echinacea Root Hexanic Extracts on Human Cancer Cell Lines." *Journal of Ethnopharmacology*, U.S. National Library of Medicine, 2007, pubmed.ncbi.nlm. nih.gov/17052874/.

Haller, Jozsef, et al. "The Anxiolytic Potential and Psychotropic Side Effects of an Echinacea Preparation in Laboratory Animals and Healthy Volunteers." *Phytotherapy Research : PTR*, U.S. National Library of Medicine, 2012, pubmed.ncbi.nlm.nih. gov/22451347/.

Liu Q;Chen Y;Shen C;Xiao Y;Wang Y;Liu Z;Liu X; "Chicoric Acid Supplementation Prevents Systemic Inflammation-Induced Memory Impairment and Amyloidogenesis via Inhibition of NF-⊠B." *FASEB Journal : Official Publication of the Federation of American Societies for Experimental Biology*, U.S. National Library of Medicine, 2017, pubmed.ncbi. nlm.nih.gov/28003341/.

Melchart, D, et al. "Immunomodulation with Echinacea - a Systematic Review of Controlled Clinical Trials." *Phytomedicine : International Journal of Phytotherapy and Phytopharmacology*, U.S. National Library of Medicine, 1994, pubmed.ncbi.nlm.nih. gov/23195946/.

Oláh A;Szabó-Papp J;Soeberdt M;Knie U;Dähnhardt-Pfeiffer S;Abels C;Bíró T; "Echinacea Purpurea-Derived Alkylamides Exhibit Potent Anti-Inflammatory Effects and Alleviate Clinical Symptoms of Atopic Eczema." *Journal of Dermatological Science*, U.S. National Library of Medicine, 2017, pubmed.ncbi.nlm.nih.gov/28610718/.

S;, Manayi A;Vazirian M;Saeidnia. "Echinacea Purpurea: Pharmacology, Phytochemistry and Analysis Methods." *Pharmacognosy Reviews*, U.S. National Library of Medicine, 2015, pubmed.ncbi.nlm.nih.gov/26009695/.

S;, Yotsawimonwat S;Rattanadechsakul J;Rattanadechsakul P;Okonogi. "Skin Improvement and Stability of Echinacea Purpurea Dermatological Formulations." *International Journal of Cosmetic Science*, U.S. National Library of Medicine, 2010, pubmed. ncbi.nlm.nih.gov/20384903/.

SD;, Chiou SY;Sung JM;Huang PW;Lin. "Antioxidant, Antidiabetic, and Antihypertensive Properties of Echinacea Purpurea Flower Extract and Caffeic Acid Derivatives Using In Vitro Models." *Journal of Medicinal Food*, U.S. National Library of Medicine, 2017, pubmed.ncbi.nlm.nih.gov/28061036/.

Shah, Sachin A, et al. "Evaluation of Echinacea for the Prevention and Treatment of the Common Cold: a Meta-Analysis." *The Lancet. Infectious Diseases*, U.S. National Library of Medicine, 2007, pubmed.ncbi.nlm.nih.gov/17597571/.

TF;, Haller J;Hohmann J;Freund. "The Effect of Echinacea Preparations in Three Laboratory Tests of Anxiety: Comparison with Chlordiazepoxide." *Phytotherapy Research : PTR*, U.S. National Library of Medicine, 2010, pubmed.ncbi.nlm.nih.gov/21031616/.

Feverfew

"Anxiolytic- and Antidepressant-like Effects of an Aqueous Extract of Tanacetum Parthenium L. Schultz-Bip (Asteraceae) in Mice." *Journal of Ethnopharmacology*, U.S. National Library of Medicine, 2016, pubmed.ncbi.nlm.nih.gov/28213105/.

Di Cesare Mannelli L;Tenci B;Zanardelli M;Maidecchi A;Lugli A;Mattoli L;Ghelardini C; "Widespread Pain Reliever Profile of a Flower Extract of Tanacetum Parthenium." *Phytomedicine : International Journal of Phytotherapy and Phytopharmacology*, U.S. National Library of Medicine, 2015, pubmed.ncbi.nlm.nih.gov/26141762/.

Feverfew (Tanacetum Parthenium L.): A Systematic Review. 2011, friendsofthewildflowergarden.org/pdfdocs/feverfewpharma.pdf.

Garlic

A;, Silagy C;Neil. "Garlic as a Lipid Lowering Agent--a Meta-Analysis." *Journal of the Royal College of Physicians of London*, U.S. National Library of Medicine, 1994, pubmed.ncbi.nlm.nih.gov/8169881/.

AA;, Ashraf R;Khan RA;Ashraf I;Qureshi. "Effects of Allium Sativum (Garlic) on Systolic and Diastolic Blood Pressure in Patients with Essential Hypertension." *Pakistan Journal of Pharmaceutical Sciences*, U.S. National Library of Medicine, 2013, pubmed.ncbi.nlm.nih.gov/24035939/.

C;, Borek. "Garlic Reduces Dementia and Heart-Disease Risk." *The Journal of Nutrition*, U.S. National Library of Medicine, 2006, pubmed.ncbi.nlm.nih.gov/16484570/.

P;, Josling. "Preventing the Common Cold with a Garlic Supplement: a Double-Blind, Placebo-Controlled Survey." *Advances in Therapy*, U.S. National Library of Medicine, 2001, pubmed.ncbi.nlm.nih.gov/11697022/.

Ginger

Altman, R D, and K C Marcussen. "Effects of a Ginger Extract on Knee Pain in Patients with Osteoarthritis." *Arthritis and Rheumatism*, U.S. National Library of Medicine, Nov. 2001, www.ncbi.nlm.nih.gov/pubmed/11710709.

F;, Ozgoli G;Goli M;Moattar. "Comparison of Effects of Ginger, Mefenamic Acid, and Ibuprofen on Pain in Women with Primary Dysmenorrhea." *Journal of Alternative and Complementary Medicine (New York, N.Y.)*, U.S. National Library of Medicine, 2009, pubmed.ncbi.nlm.nih.gov/19216660/.

Maghbooli M;Golipour F;Moghimi Esfandabadi A;Yousefi M; "Comparison between the Efficacy of Ginger and Sumatriptan in the Ablative Treatment of the Common Migraine." *Phytotherapy Research : PTR*, U.S. National Library of Medicine, 2014, pubmed.ncbi.nlm. nih.gov/23657930/.

Ryan JL;Heckler CE;Roscoe JA;Dakhil SR;Kirshner J;Flynn PJ;Hickok JT;Morrow GR; "Ginger (Zingiber Officinale) Reduces Acute Chemotherapy-Induced Nausea: a URCC CCOP Study of 576 Patients." *Supportive Care in Cancer : Official Journal of the Multinational Association of Supportive Care in Cancer*, U.S. National Library of Medicine, 2012, pubmed.ncbi.nlm.nih.gov/21818642/.

Globe Artichoke

AF;, Roghani-Dehkordi F;Kamkhah. "Artichoke Leaf Juice Contains Antihypertensive Effect in Patients with Mild Hypertension." *Journal of Dietary Supplements*, U.S. National Library of Medicine, 2009, pubmed.ncbi.nlm.nih.gov/22435514/.

Ben Salem M;Affes H;Ksouda K;Dhouibi R;Sahnoun Z;Hammami S;Zeghal KM; "Pharmacological Studies of Artichoke Leaf Extract and Their Health Benefits." *Plant Foods for Human Nutrition (Dordrecht, Netherlands)*, U.S. National Library of Medicine, 2015, pubmed.ncbi.nlm.nih.gov/26310198/.

E;, Wider B;Pittler MH;Thompson-Coon J;Ernst. "Artichoke Leaf Extract for Treating Hypercholesterolaemia." *The Cochrane Database of Systematic Reviews*, U.S. National Library of Medicine, 2013, pubmed.ncbi.nlm.nih.gov/23543518/.

Great Burdock

Chan, Yuk-Shing, et al. "A Review of the Pharmacological Effects of Arctium Lappa (Burdock)." *Inflammopharmacology*, SP Birkhäuser Verlag Basel, 28 Oct. 2010, link.springer.com/article/10.1007/s10787-010-0062-4.

González-Molina, E., et al. "Natural Bioactive Compounds of Citrus Limon for Food and Health." *Journal of Pharmaceutical and Biomedical Analysis*, Elsevier, 29 July 2009, www.sciencedirect.com/science/article/abs/pii/S0731708509004816.

Maghsoumi-Norouzabad, Leila, et al. "Effects of Arctium Lappa L. (Burdock) Root Tea on Inflammatory Status and Oxidative Stress in Patients with Knee Osteoarthritis." *Wiley Online Library*, John Wiley & Sons, Ltd, 28 Oct. 2014, onlinelibrary.wiley.com/doi/abs/10.1111/1756-185X.12477.

Predes, Fabricia S, et al. "Antioxidative and in Vitro Antiproliferative Activity of Arctium Lappa Root Extracts." *BMC Complementary and Alternative Medicine*, BioMed Central, 23 Mar. 2011, www.ncbi.nlm.nih.gov/pmc/articles/PMC3073957/.

RK;, Miglani A;Manchanda. "Observational Study of Arctium Lappa in the Treatment of Acne Vulgaris." *Homeopathy : the Journal of the Faculty of Homeopathy*, U.S. National Library of Medicine, 2014, pubmed.ncbi.nlm.nih.gov/24931753/.

Great Mullein

Mahdavi S;Amiradalat M;Babashpour M;Sheikhlooei H;Miransari M; "The Antioxidant, Anticarcinogenic and Antimicrobial Properties of Verbascum Thapsus L." *Medicinal Chemistry (Shariqah (United Arab Emirates))*, U.S. National Library of Medicine, 2020, pubmed.ncbi.nlm.nih.gov/31456524/.

Rajbhandari, M, et al. "Antiviral Activity of Some Plants Used in Nepalese Traditional Medicine." *Evidence-Based Complementary and Alternative Medicine : ECAM*, Oxford University Press, Dec. 2009, www.ncbi.nlm.nih.gov/pmc/articles/PMC2781767/\.

Serkedjieva, Julia. "Combined Anti Influenza Virus Activity of Flos Verbasci Infusion and Amantadine Derivatives." *Wiley Online Library*, John Wiley & Sons, Ltd, 23 Oct. 2000, onlinelibrary.wiley.com/doi/abs/10.1002/1099-1573%28200011%2914%3A7%3C571%3A%3AAID-PTR653%3E3.0.CO%3B2-A.

Jasmine

Chen W;Zhang Z;Shen Y;Duan X;Jiang Y; "Effect of Tea Polyphenols on Lipid Peroxidation and Antioxidant Activity of Litchi (Litchi Chinensis Sonn.) Fruit during Cold Storage." *Molecules (Basel, Switzerland)*, U.S. National Library of Medicine, 2014, pubmed.ncbi.nlm.nih.gov/25335111/.

Hursel R;Viechtbauer W;Dulloo AG;Tremblay A;Tappy L;Rumpler W;Westerterp-Plantenga MS; "The Effects of Catechin Rich Teas and Caffeine on Energy Expenditure and Fat Oxidation: a Meta-Analysis." *Obesity Reviews : an Official Journal of the International Association for the Study of Obesity*, U.S. National Library of Medicine, 2011, pubmed.ncbi.nlm.nih.gov/21366839/.

Kumar H;Lim HW;More SV;Kim BW;Koppula S;Kim IS;Choi DK; "The Role of Free Radicals in the Aging Brain and Parkinson's Disease: Convergence and Parallelism." *International Journal of Molecular Sciences*, U.S. National Library of Medicine, 2012, pubmed.ncbi.nlm.nih.gov/22949875/.

Lodhia P;Yaegaki K;Khakbaznejad A;Imai T;Sato T;Tanaka T;Murata T;Kamoda T; "Effect of Green Tea on Volatile Sulfur Compounds in Mouth Air." *Journal of Nutritional Science and Vitaminology*, U.S. National Library of Medicine, 2008, pubmed.ncbi.nlm.nih. gov/18388413/.

M;, Cappelletti S;Piacentino D;Sani G;Aromatario. "Caffeine: Cognitive and Physical Performance Enhancer or Psychoactive Drug?" *Current Neuropharmacology*, U.S. National Library of Medicine, 2015, pubmed.ncbi.nlm.nih.gov/26074744/.

MM;, Anderson RA;Polansky. "Tea Enhances Insulin Activity." *Journal of Agricultural and Food Chemistry*, U.S. National Library of Medicine, 2002, pubmed.ncbi.nlm.nih. gov/12428980/.

N;, Vinson JA;Teufel K;Wu. "Green and Black Teas Inhibit Atherosclerosis by Lipid, Antioxidant, and Fibrinolytic Mechanisms." *Journal of Agricultural and Food Chemistry*, U.S. National Library of Medicine, 2004, pubmed.ncbi.nlm.nih.gov/15161246/.

Pang J;Zhang Z;Zheng TZ;Bassig BA;Mao C;Liu X;Zhu Y;Shi K;Ge J;Yang YJ;Dejia-Huang None;Bai M;Peng Y; "Green Tea Consumption and Risk of Cardiovascular and Ischemic Related Diseases: A Meta-Analysis." *International Journal of Cardiology*, U.S. National Library of Medicine, 2016, pubmed.ncbi.nlm.nih.gov/26318390/.

S;, Hirasawa M;Takada K;Otake. "Inhibition of Acid Production in Dental Plaque Bacteria by Green Tea Catechins." *Caries Research*, U.S. National Library of Medicine, 2006, pubmed.ncbi.nlm.nih.gov/16707877/.

WW;, Huang WJ;Zhang X;Chen. "Role of Oxidative Stress in Alzheimer's Disease." *Biomedical Reports*, U.S. National Library of Medicine, 2016, pubmed.ncbi.nlm.nih. gov/27123241/.

Jiaogulan

By. "JIAOGULAN.ORG." *Jiaogulanorg*, 1 June 1970, www.jiaogulan.org/category/jiaogulan-research/.

Chou SC;Chen KW;Hwang JS;Lu WT;Chu YY;Lin JD;Chang HJ;See LC; "The Add-on Effects of Gynostemma Pentaphyllum on Nonalcoholic Fatty Liver Disease." *Alternative Therapies in Health and Medicine*, U.S. National Library of Medicine, 2006, pubmed.ncbi.nlm.nih.gov/16708768/.

Johnny Jump-Up

Hellinger, Roland, et al. "Immunosuppressive Activity of an Aqueous Viola Tricolor Herbal Extract." *Journal of Ethnopharmacology*, U.S. National Library of Medicine, 2014, www.ncbi.nlm.nih.gov/pmc/articles/PMC3918579/#:~:text=Due%20to%20its%20 anti%2Dinflammatory,such%20as%20bronchitis%20or%20asthma.

Lamb's Ear

Türkiye, Gebze-Kocaeli. "Use of Stachys Species (Mountain Tea) as Herbal Tea and Food Ahmet C. Göⓧ." *ACG Publications*, TÜBİTAK UME, Chemistry Group, Organic Chemistry Laboratory, P, 2013, www.acgpubs.org/doc/2018080911510113-RNP-1312-489.pdf.

Bahadori, Mir Babak, et al. "The Health Benefits of Three Hedgenettle Herbal Teas (Stachys Byzantina, Stachys Inflata, and Stachys Lavandulifolia) - Profiling Phenolic and Antioxidant Activities." *European Journal of Integrative Medicine*, Urban & Fischer, 18 May 2020, www.sciencedirect.com/science/article/abs/pii/S1876382020300342.

Saeedi, M, et al. "Antimicrobial Studies on Extracts of Four Species of Stachys." *Indian Journal of Pharmaceutical Sciences*, Medknow Publications, 2008, www.ncbi.nlm.nih.gov/pmc/articles/PMC2792521/.

Lavender

Cavanagh, H. M. A., and J. M. Wilkinson. "Biological Activities of Lavender Essential Oil." *Wiley Online Library*, John Wiley & Sons, Ltd, 11 June 2002, onlinelibrary.wiley.com/doi/abs/10.1002/ptr.1103.

Han SH;Hur MH;Buckle J;Choi J;Lee MS; "Effect of Aromatherapy on Symptoms of Dysmenorrhea in College Students: A Randomized Placebo-Controlled Clinical Trial." *Journal of Alternative and Complementary Medicine (New York, N.Y.)*, U.S. National Library of Medicine, 2006, pubmed.ncbi.nlm.nih.gov/16884344/.

Koulivand, Peir Hossein, et al. "Lavender and the Nervous System." *Evidence-Based Complementary and Alternative Medicine : ECAM*, Hindawi Publishing Corporation, 2013, www.ncbi.nlm.nih.gov/pmc/articles/PMC3612440/.

Lehrner, J., et al. "Ambient Odors of Orange and Lavender Reduce Anxiety and Improve Mood in a Dental Office." *Physiology & Behavior*, Elsevier, 10 Aug. 2005, www.sciencedirect.com/science/article/abs/pii/S0031938405002660.

Orchard, Ané, and Sandy van Vuuren. "Commercial Essential Oils as Potential Antimicrobials to Treat Skin Diseases." *Evidence-Based Complementary and Alternative Medicine : ECAM*, Hindawi, 2017, www.ncbi.nlm.nih.gov/pmc/articles/PMC5435909/.

Lemon Balm

Kennedy, D.O, et al. *Modulation of Mood and Cognitive Performance Following ACUTE Administration of Melissa Officinalis (Lemon Balm)*. 29 Apr. 2002, www.sciencedirect.com/science/article/abs/pii/S0091305702007773.

Scholey, Andrew, et al. *Anti-Stress Effects of Lemon Balm-Containing Foods*. 30 Oct. 2014, www.mdpi.com/2072-6643/6/11/4805.

YUI, Shintaro, et al. *Beneficial Effects of Lemon Balm Leaf Extract on in Vitro Glycation of Proteins, Arterial Stiffness, and Skin Elasticity in Healthy Adults*. 28 Mar. 2017, www.jstage.jst.go.jp/article/jnsv/63/1/63_59/_article/-char/ja/.

Lemongrass

Chaudhari LK;Jawale BA;Sharma S;Sharma H;Kumar CD;Kulkarni PA; "Antimicrobial Activity of Commercially Available Essential Oils against Streptococcus Mutans." *The Journal of Contemporary Dental Practice*, U.S. National Library of Medicine, 2012, pubmed.ncbi.nlm.nih.gov/22430697/.

Fernandes, Cn, et al. "Investigation of the Mechanisms Underlying the Gastroprotective Effect of Cymbopogon Citratus Essential Oil." *Journal of Young Pharmacists : JYP*, Medknow Publications & Media Pvt Ltd, Jan. 2012, www.ncbi.nlm.nih.gov/pmc/articles/PMC3326778/.

Shah, Gagan, et al. "Scientific Basis for the Therapeutic Use of Cymbopogon Citratus, Stapf (Lemon Grass)." *Journal of Advanced Pharmaceutical Technology & Research*, Medknow Publications Pvt Ltd, Jan. 2011, www.ncbi.nlm.nih.gov/pmc/articles/PMC3217679/.

Marsh Mallow

Banaee, Mahdi, et al. "Therapeutic Effects of Marshmallow (Althaea Officinalis L.) Extract on Plasma Biochemical Parameters of Common Carp Infected with Aeromonas Hydrophila." Veterinary Research Forum : an International Quarterly Journal, Urmia University Press, 2017, www.ncbi.nlm.nih.gov/pmc/articles/PMC5524553/.

Bonaterra, Gabriel A, et al. "Anti-Inflammatory and Anti-Oxidative Effects of Phytohustil® and Root Extract of Althaea Officinalis L. on Macrophages in Vitro." Frontiers in Pharmacology, Frontiers Media S.A., 17 Mar. 2020, www.ncbi.nlm.nih.gov/pmc/articles/PMC7090173/.

Dawid-Pać, Renata. "Review PaperMedicinal Plants Used in Treatment of Inflammatory Skin Diseases." Advances in Dermatology and Allergology/Postępy Dermatologii i Alergologii, Termedia, 20 June 2013, www.termedia.pl/Review-paper-Medicinal-plants-used-in-treatment-of-inflammatory-skin-diseases,7,20954,0,1.html.

Yarnell, Eric. "Althaea Officinalis." Althaea Officinalis - an Overview | ScienceDirect Topics, 2007, www.sciencedirect.com/topics/agricultural-and-biological-sciences/althaea-officinalis.

Meadowsweet

Bespalov VG;Alexandrov VA;Vysochina GI;Kostikova VA;Semenov AL;Baranenko DA; "Inhibitory Effect of Filipendula Ulmaria on Mammary Carcinogenesis Induced by Local Administration of Methylnitrosourea to Target Organ in Rats." *Anti-Cancer Agents in Medicinal Chemistry*, U.S. National Library of Medicine, 2018, pubmed.ncbi.nlm.nih.gov/29607788/.

Katanić J;Boroja T;Mihailović V;Nikles S;Pan SP;Rosić G;Selaković D;Joksimović J;Mitrović S;Bauer R; "In Vitro and in Vivo Assessment of Meadowsweet (Filipendula Ulmaria) as Anti-Inflammatory Agent." *Journal of Ethnopharmacology*, U.S. National Library of Medicine, 2016, pubmed.ncbi.nlm.nih.gov/27721054/.

Katanić J;Boroja T;Stanković N;Mihailović V;Mladenović M;Kreft S;Vrvić MM; "Bioactivity, Stability and Phenolic Characterization of Filipendula Ulmaria (L.) Maxim." *Food & Function*, U.S. National Library of Medicine, 2015, pubmed.ncbi.nlm.nih.gov/25695410/.

Olennikov, Daniil N, et al. "Meadowsweet Teas as New Functional Beverages: Comparative Analysis of Nutrients, Phytochemicals and Biological Effects of Four Filipendula Species." *Molecules (Basel, Switzerland)*, MDPI, 26 Dec. 2016, www.ncbi.nlm.nih.gov/pmc/articles/PMC6155584/.

Motherwort

Easley, T. (2016, December 5). *Motherwort*. Eclectic School of Herbal Medicine. https://www.eclecticschoolofherbalmedicine.com/motherwort/.

Fierascu, R. C., Fierascu, I., Ortan, A., Fierascu, I. C., Anuta, V., Velescu, B. S., Pituru, S. M., & Dinu-Pirvu, C. E. (2019, April 17). *Leonurus cardiaca L. as a Source of Bioactive Compounds: An Update of the European Medicines Agency Assessment Report (2010)*. BioMed research international. https://www.ncbi.nlm.nih.gov/pmc/articles/PMC6500680/.

Shikov AN;Pozharitskaya ON;Makarov VG;Demchenko DV;Shikh EV; (n.d.). *Effect of Leonurus cardiaca oil extract in patients with arterial hypertension accompanied by anxiety and sleep disorders*. Phytotherapy research : PTR. https://pubmed.ncbi.nlm.nih.gov/20839214/.

Nasturtium

Jakubczyk K;Janda K;Watychowicz K;Łukasiak J;Wolska J; "Garden Nasturtium (Tropaeolum Majus L.) - a Source of Mineral Elements and Bioactive Compounds." *Roczniki Panstwowego Zakladu Higieny*, U.S. National Library of Medicine, 2018, pubmed.ncbi.nlm.nih.gov/29766690/.

Navarro-González, Inmaculada, et al. "Nutritional Composition and Antioxidant Capacity in Edible Flowers: Characterisation of Phenolic Compounds by HPLC-DAD-ESI/MSn." *International Journal of Molecular Sciences*, MDPI, 31 Dec. 2014, www.ncbi.nlm.nih.gov/pmc/articles/PMC4307276/.

Oregano

D;, Lagouri V;Boskou. "Nutrient Antioxidants in Oregano." *International Journal of Food Sciences and Nutrition*, U.S. National Library of Medicine, 1996, pubmed.ncbi.nlm.nih.gov/8933203/.

Fan K;Li X;Cao Y;Qi H;Li L;Zhang Q;Sun H; "Carvacrol Inhibits Proliferation and Induces Apoptosis in Human Colon Cancer Cells." *Anti-Cancer Drugs*, U.S. National Library of Medicine, 2015, pubmed.ncbi.nlm.nih.gov/26214321/.

KR;, Gilling DH;Kitajima M;Torrey JR;Bright. "Antiviral Efficacy and Mechanisms of Action of Oregano Essential Oil and Its Primary Component Carvacrol against Murine Norovirus." *Journal of Applied Microbiology*, U.S. National Library of Medicine, 2014, pubmed.ncbi.nlm.nih.gov/24779581/.

P;, Saeed S;Tariq. "Antibacterial Activity of Oregano (Origanum Vulgare Linn.) against Gram Positive Bacteria." *Pakistan Journal of Pharmaceutical Sciences*, U.S. National Library of Medicine, 2009, pubmed.ncbi.nlm.nih.gov/19783523.

Parsley

Charles, D.J. "Parsley." *Parsley - an Overview | ScienceDirect Topics*, 2012, www.sciencedirect.com/topics/agricultural-and-biological-sciences/parsley.

Farzaei MH;Abbasabadi Z;Ardekani MR;Rahimi R;Farzaei F; "Parsley: a Review of Ethnopharmacology, Phytochemistry and Biological Activities." *Journal of Traditional Chinese Medicine = Chung i Tsa Chih Ying Wen Pan*, U.S. National Library of Medicine, 2013, pubmed.ncbi.nlm.nih.gov/24660617/.

Passion Flower

Fonseca, Lyca R. da, et al. "Herbal Medicinal Products from Passiflora for Anxiety: An Unexploited Potential." *The Scientific World Journal*, Hindawi, 20 July 2020, www.hindawi.com/journals/tswj/2020/6598434/.

Kim, Mijiin, et al. *Role Identification of Passiflora Incarnata Linnaeus: A Mini Review.* Journal of Menopausal Women, 2017, synapse.koreamed.org/upload/SynapseData/PDFData/3165jmm/jmm-23-156.pdf.

Ngan, A., and R. Conduit. "A Double-Blind, Placebo-Controlled Investigation of the Effects of Passiflora Incarnata (Passionflower) Herbal Tea on Subjective Sleep Quality." *Wiley Online Library*, John Wiley & Sons, Ltd, 3 Feb. 2011, onlinelibrary.wiley.com/doi/abs/10.1002/ptr.3400.

Peppermint

From the Division of Pediatric and Adolescent Dermatology. "Mentha Piperita (Peppermint) : Dermatitis." *LWW*, 2010, journals.lww.com/dermatitis/Abstract/2010/11000/Mentha_piperita__Peppermint_.5.aspx.

Lucy I. Spirling, Ian R. Daniels. "Botanical Perspectives on Health Peppermint: More than Just an after-Dinner Mint - Lucy I. Spirling, Ian R. Daniels, 2001." *SAGE Journals*, 2001, journals.sagepub.com/doi/abs/10.1177/146642400112100113.

McKay, Diane L., and Jeffrey B. Blumberg. "A Review of the Bioactivity and Potential Health Benefits of Peppermint Tea (Mentha Piperita L.)." *Wiley Online Library*, John Wiley & Sons, Ltd, 12 June 2006, onlinelibrary.wiley.com/doi/abs/10.1002/ptr.1936.

Nayak, Parv, et al. *Peppermint a Medicinal Herb and Treasure of Health: A Review.* Journal of Pharmacognosy and Phytochemistry, 2020, www.phytojournal.com/archives/2020/vol9issue3/PartY/9-3-248-685.pdf.

Nolkemper S;Reichling J;Stintzing FC;Carle R;Schnitzler P; "Antiviral Effect of Aqueous Extracts from Species of the Lamiaceae Family against Herpes Simplex Virus Type 1 and Type 2 in Vitro." *Planta Medica*, U.S. National Library of Medicine, 2006, pubmed.ncbi.nlm.nih.gov/17091431/.

Riachi, Liza G., and Carlos A.B. De Maria. "Peppermint Antioxidants Revisited." *Food Chemistry*, Elsevier, 17 Dec. 2014, www.sciencedirect.com/science/article/abs/pii/S030881461401930X.

Purslane

Rahimi, Vafa Baradaran, et al. "A Pharmacological Review on *Portulaca Oleracea* L.: Focusing on Anti-Inflammatory, Anti- Oxidant, Immuno-Modulatory and Antitumor Activities." *Journal of Pharmacopuncture*, The Korean Pharmacopuncture Institute (KPI), Mar. 2019, www.ncbi.nlm.nih.gov/pmc/articles/PMC6461301/.

Uddin, Md Kamal, et al. "Purslane Weed (Portulaca Oleracea): a Prospective Plant Source of Nutrition, Omega-3 Fatty Acid, and Antioxidant Attributes." *TheScientificWorldJournal*, Hindawi Publishing Corporation, 10 Feb. 2014, www.ncbi.nlm.nih.gov/pmc/articles/PMC3934766/.

Red Clover

Atkinson C;Compston JE;Day NE;Dowsett M;Bingham SA; "The Effects of Phytoestrogen Isoflavones on Bone Density in Women: a Double-Blind, Randomized, Placebo-Controlled Trial." *The American Journal of Clinical Nutrition*, U.S. National Library of Medicine, 2004, pubmed.ncbi.nlm.nih.gov/14749241/.

Ehsanpour, Soheila, et al. "The Effects of Red Clover on Quality of Life in Post-Menopausal Women." *Iranian Journal of Nursing and Midwifery Research*, Medknow Publications & Media Pvt Ltd, Jan. 2012, www.ncbi.nlm.nih.gov/pmc/articles/PMC3590693/.

Ghazanfarpour M;Sadeghi R;Roudsari RL;Khorsand I;Khadivzadeh T;Muoio B; "Red Clover for Treatment of Hot Flashes and Menopausal Symptoms: A Systematic Review and Meta-Analysis." *Journal of Obstetrics and Gynaecology : the Journal of the Institute of Obstetrics and Gynaecology*, U.S. National Library of Medicine, 2016, pubmed.ncbi.nlm.nih.gov/26471215/.

Lipovac, Markus, et al. "Effect of Red Clover Isoflavones over Skin, Appendages, and Mucosal Status in Postmenopausal Women." *Obstetrics and Gynecology International*, Hindawi Publishing Corporation, 2011, www.ncbi.nlm.nih.gov/pmc/articles/PMC3206499/.

Sansai K;Na Takuathung M;Khatsri R;Teekachunhatean S;Hanprasertpong N;Koonrungsesomboon N; "Effects of Isoflavone Interventions on Bone Mineral Density in Postmenopausal Women: a Systematic Review and Meta-Analysis of Randomized Controlled Trials." *Osteoporosis International : a Journal Established as Result of Cooperation between the European Foundation for Osteoporosis and the National Osteoporosis Foundation of the USA*, U.S. National Library of Medicine, 2020, pubmed.ncbi.nlm.nih.gov/32524173/.

Thorup, Anne Cathrine, et al. "Intake of Novel Red Clover Supplementation for 12 Weeks Improves Bone Status in Healthy Menopausal Women." *Evidence-Based Complementary and Alternative Medicine : ECAM*, Hindawi Publishing Corporation, 2015, www.ncbi.nlm.nih.gov/pmc/articles/PMC4523657/.

Rosemary

Andrade, Joana M, et al. "*Rosmarinus Officinalis* L.: an Update Review of Its Phytochemistry and Biological Activity." *Future Science OA*, Future Science Ltd, 1 Feb. 2018, www.ncbi.nlm.nih.gov/pmc/articles/PMC5905578/.

Chemerovski-Glikman, Marina, et al. "Rosmarinic Acid Restores Complete Transparency of Sonicated Human Cataract Ex Vivo and Delays Cataract Formation In Vivo." *Scientific Reports*, Nature Publishing Group UK, 19 June 2018, www.ncbi.nlm.nih.gov/pmc/articles/PMC6008418/.

Habtemariam, Solomon. "The Therapeutic Potential of Rosemary (Rosmarinus Officinalis) Diterpenes for Alzheimer's Disease." *Evidence-Based Complementary and Alternative Medicine : ECAM*, Hindawi Publishing Corporation, 2016, www.ncbi.nlm.nih.gov/pmc/articles/PMC4749867/.

Naimi, Madina, et al. "Rosemary Extract as a Potential Anti-Hyperglycemic Agent: Current Evidence and Future Perspectives." *Nutrients*, MDPI, 1 Sept. 2017, www.ncbi.nlm.nih.gov/pmc/articles/PMC5622728/.

Ou J;Huang J;Zhao D;Du B;Wang M; "Protective Effect of Rosmarinic Acid and Carnosic Acid against Streptozotocin-Induced Oxidation, Glycation, Inflammation and Microbiota Imbalance in Diabetic Rats." *Food & Function*, U.S. National Library of Medicine, 2018, pubmed.ncbi.nlm.nih.gov/29372208/.

Sage

Beheshti-Rouy M;Azarsina M;Rezaie-Soufi L;Alikhani MY;Roshanaie G;Komaki S; "The Antibacterial Effect of Sage Extract (Salvia Officinalis) Mouthwash against Streptococcus Mutans in Dental Plaque: a Randomized Clinical Trial." *Iranian Journal of Microbiology*, U.S. National Library of Medicine, 2015, pubmed.ncbi.nlm.nih.gov/26668706/.

Ben Khedher MR;Hammami M;Arch JRS;Hislop DC;Eze D;Wargent ET;Kępczyńska MA;Zaibi MS; "Preventive Effects of Salvia Officinalis Leaf Extract on Insulin Resistance and Inflammation in a Model of High Fat Diet-Induced Obesity in Mice That Responds to Rosiglitazone." *PeerJ*, U.S. National Library of Medicine, 2018, pubmed.ncbi.nlm.nih.gov/29333341/.

LY;, Lu Y;Foo. "Polyphenolics of Salvia--a Review." *Phytochemistry*, U.S. National Library of Medicine, 2002, pubmed.ncbi.nlm.nih.gov/11809447/.

M;, Ghorbani A;Esmaeilizadeh. "Pharmacological Properties of Salvia Officinalis and Its Components." *Journal of Traditional and Complementary Medicine*, U.S. National Library of Medicine, 2017, pubmed.ncbi.nlm.nih.gov/29034191/.

Park JE;Lee KE;Jung E;Kang S;Kim YJ; "Sclareol Isolated from Salvia Officinalis Improves Facial Wrinkles via an Antiphotoaging Mechanism." *Journal of Cosmetic Dermatology*, U.S. National Library of Medicine, 2016, pubmed.ncbi.nlm.nih.gov/27466023/.

R;, Kargozar R;Azizi H;Salari. "A Review of Effective Herbal Medicines in Controlling Menopausal Symptoms." *Electronic Physician*, U.S. National Library of Medicine, 2017, pubmed.ncbi.nlm.nih.gov/29403626/.

Sá CM;Ramos AA;Azevedo MF;Lima CF;Fernandes-Ferreira M;Pereira-Wilson C; "Sage Tea Drinking Improves Lipid Profile and Antioxidant Defences in Humans." *International Journal of Molecular Sciences*, U.S. National Library of Medicine, 2009, pubmed.ncbi.nlm.nih.gov/19865527/.

Spearmint

Akdoğan M;Tamer MN;Cüre E;Cüre MC;Köroğlu BK;Delibaş N; "Effect of Spearmint (Mentha Spicata Labiatae) Teas on Androgen Levels in Women with Hirsutism." *Phytotherapy Research : PTR*, U.S. National Library of Medicine, 2007, pubmed.ncbi.nlm. nih.gov/17310494/.

Bardaweel SK;Bakchiche B;ALSalamat HA;Rezzoug M;Gherib A;Flamini G; "Chemical Composition, Antioxidant, Antimicrobial and Antiproliferative Activities of Essential Oil of Mentha Spicata L. (Lamiaceae) from Algerian Saharan Atlas." *BMC Complementary and Alternative Medicine*, U.S. National Library of Medicine, 2018, pubmed.ncbi.nlm.nih. gov/29970065/.

Cirlini M;Mena P;Tassotti M;Herrlinger KA;Nieman KM;Dall'Asta C;Del Rio D; "Phenolic and Volatile Composition of a Dry Spearmint (Mentha Spicata L.) Extract." *Molecules (Basel, Switzerland)*, U.S. National Library of Medicine, 2016, pubmed.ncbi.nlm. nih.gov/27527127/.

M;, Farid O;El Haidani A;Eddouks. "Antidiabetic Effect of Spearmint in Streptozotocin-Induced Diabetic Rats." *Endocrine, Metabolic & Immune Disorders Drug Targets*, U.S. National Library of Medicine, 2018, pubmed.ncbi.nlm.nih.gov/29769013/.

Souza FV;da Rocha MB;de Souza DP;Marçal RM; "(-)-Carvone: Antispasmodic Effect and Mode of Action." *Fitoterapia*, U.S. National Library of Medicine, 2013, pubmed.ncbi. nlm.nih.gov/23103297/.

St. John's Wort

Berner, Linde K. *St. John's Wort for Treating Depression.*, Cochrane, www.cochrane.org/ CD000448/DEPRESSN_st.-johns-wort-for-treating-depression.

Canning S;Waterman M;Orsi N;Ayres J;Simpson N;Dye L; "The Efficacy of Hypericum Perforatum (St John's Wort) for the Treatment of Premenstrual Syndrome: a Randomized, Double-Blind, Placebo-Controlled Trial." *CNS Drugs*, U.S. National Library of Medicine, 2010, pubmed.ncbi.nlm.nih.gov/20155996/.

CM;, Wölfle U;Seelinger G;Schempp. "Topical Application of St. John's Wort (Hypericum Perforatum)." *Planta Medica*, U.S. National Library of Medicine, 2014, pubmed.ncbi.nlm. nih.gov/24214835/.

CY;, Ng QX;Venkatanarayanan N;Ho. "Clinical Use of Hypericum Perforatum (St John's Wort) in Depression: A Meta-Analysis." *Journal of Affective Disorders*, U.S. National Library of Medicine, 2017, pubmed.ncbi.nlm.nih.gov/28064110/.

O;, Yücel A;Kan Y;Yesilada E;Akın. "Effect of St.John's Wort (Hypericum Perforatum) Oily Extract for the Care and Treatment of Pressure Sores; a Case Report." *Journal of Ethnopharmacology*, U.S. National Library of Medicine, 2017, pubmed.ncbi.nlm.nih. gov/28011162/.

Stevia
....

A;, Paul S;Sengupta S;Bandyopadhyay TK;Bhattacharyya. "Stevioside Induced ROS-Mediated Apoptosis through Mitochondrial Pathway in Human Breast Cancer Cell Line MCF-7." *Nutrition and Cancer*, U.S. National Library of Medicine, 2012, pubmed.ncbi. nlm.nih.gov/23061910/.

Ahmad, Uswa, et al. "Antihyperlipidemic Efficacy of Aqueous Extract of Stevia Rebaudiana Bertoni in Albino Rats." *Lipids in Health and Disease*, BioMed Central, 27 July 2018, www.ncbi.nlm.nih.gov/pmc/articles/PMC6064095/.

Anton, Stephen D, et al. "Effects of Stevia, Aspartame, and Sucrose on Food Intake, Satiety, and Postprandial Glucose and Insulin Levels." *Appetite*, U.S. National Library of Medicine, Aug. 2010, www.ncbi.nlm.nih.gov/pmc/articles/PMC2900484/.

Chen, Junming, et al. "Steviol, a Natural Product Inhibits Proliferation of the Gastrointestinal Cancer Cells Intensively." *Oncotarget*, Impact Journals LLC, 29 May 2018, www.ncbi.nlm.nih.gov/pmc/articles/PMC5995179/.

Stinging Nettles

Domola MS;Vu V;Robson-Doucette CA;Sweeney G;Wheeler MB; "Insulin Mimetics in Urtica Dioica: Structural and Computational Analyses of Urtica Dioica Extracts." *Phytotherapy Research : PTR*, U.S. National Library of Medicine, 2010, pubmed.ncbi.nlm.nih.gov/20013820/.

K;, Riehemann K;Behnke B;Schulze-Osthoff. "Plant Extracts from Stinging Nettle (Urtica Dioica), an Antirheumatic Remedy, Inhibit the Proinflammatory Transcription Factor NF-KappaB." *FEBS Letters*, U.S. National Library of Medicine, 1999, pubmed.ncbi.nlm.nih.gov/9923611/.

Qayyum R;Qamar HM;Khan S;Salma U;Khan T;Shah AJ; "Mechanisms Underlying the Antihypertensive Properties of Urtica Dioica." *Journal of Translational Medicine*, U.S. National Library of Medicine, 2016, pubmed.ncbi.nlm.nih.gov/27585814/.

Zouari Bouassida K;Bardaa S;Khimiri M;Rebaii T;Tounsi S;Jlaiel L;Trigui M; "Exploring the Urtica Dioica Leaves Hemostatic and Wound-Healing Potential." *BioMed Research International*, U.S. National Library of Medicine, 2017, pubmed.ncbi.nlm.nih.gov/29201895/.

Sunflower

Adeleke, Bartholomew Saanu, and Olubukola Oluranti Babalola. "Oilseed Crop Sunflower (*Helianthus Annuus*) as a Source of Food: Nutritional and Health Benefits." *Food Science & Nutrition*, John Wiley and Sons Inc., 31 July 2020, www.ncbi.nlm.nih.gov/pmc/articles/PMC7500752/.

Anwar, DA, et al. "Welcome to CAB Direct." *CAB Direct*, Horticulture Dept., Fac. of Agric., Ain Shams University, Shoubra El-Kheima, Cairo, Egypt., 2009, www.cabdirect.org/cabdirect/abstract/20093248180.

Guo, Shuangshuang, et al. "A Review of Phytochemistry, Metabolite Changes, and Medicinal Uses of the Common Sunflower Seed and Sprouts (Helianthus Annuus L.)." *BMC Chemistry*, Springer International Publishing, 29 Sept. 2017, bmcchem.biomedcentral.com/articles/10.1186/s13065-017-0328-7.

Pal, Dilipkumar. "Sunflower (Helianthus Annuus L.) Seeds in Health and Nutrition." *Nuts and Seeds in Health and Disease Prevention*, Academic Press, 8 Apr. 2011, www.sciencedirect.com/science/article/pii/B9780123756886101306.

Tarragon
·····················

dela Peña IJ;Hong E;Kim HJ;de la Peña JB;Woo TS;Lee YS;Cheong JH; "Artemisia Capillaris Thunberg Produces Sedative-Hypnotic Effects in Mice, Which Are Probably Mediated Through Potentiation of the GABAA Receptor." *The American Journal of Chinese Medicine*, U.S. National Library of Medicine, 2015, pubmed.ncbi.nlm.nih.gov/26119953/.

G;, Maham M;Moslemzadeh H;Jalilzadeh-Amin. "Antinociceptive Effect of the Essential Oil of Tarragon (Artemisia Dracunculus)." *Pharmaceutical Biology*, U.S. National Library of Medicine, 2013, pubmed.ncbi.nlm.nih.gov/24074293/.

Horning KJ;Caito SW;Tipps KG;Bowman AB;Aschner M; "Manganese Is Essential for Neuronal Health." *Annual Review of Nutrition*, U.S. National Library of Medicine, 2015, pubmed.ncbi.nlm.nih.gov/25974698/.

Méndez-Del Villar M;Puebla-Pérez AM;Sánchez-Peña MJ;González-Ortiz LJ;Martínez-Abundis E;González-Ortiz M; "Effect of Artemisia Dracunculus Administration on Glycemic Control, Insulin Sensitivity, and Insulin Secretion in Patients with Impaired Glucose Tolerance." *Journal of Medicinal Food*, U.S. National Library of Medicine, 2016, pubmed.ncbi.nlm.nih.gov/27097076/.

Raeisi M;Tajik H;Razavi RS;Maham M;Moradi M;Hajimohammadi B;Naghili H;Hashemi M;Mehdizadeh T; "Essential Oil of Tarragon (Artemisia Dracunculus) Antibacterial Activity on Staphylococcus Aureus and Escherichia Coli in Culture Media and Iranian White Cheese." *Iranian Journal of Microbiology*, U.S. National Library of Medicine, 2012, pubmed.ncbi.nlm.nih.gov/22783458/.

Ribnicky DM;Poulev A;Watford M;Cefalu WT;Raskin I; "Antihyperglycemic Activity of Tarralin, an Ethanolic Extract of Artemisia Dracunculus L." *Phytomedicine : International Journal of Phytotherapy and Phytopharmacology*, U.S. National Library of Medicine, 2006, pubmed.ncbi.nlm.nih.gov/16920509/.

Thyme

H;, Kemmerich B;Eberhardt R;Stammer. "Efficacy and Tolerability of a Fluid Extract Combination of Thyme Herb and Ivy Leaves and Matched Placebo in Adults Suffering from Acute Bronchitis with Productive Cough. A Prospective, Double-Blind, Placebo-Controlled Clinical Trial." *Arzneimittel-Forschung*, U.S. National Library of Medicine, 2006, pubmed.ncbi.nlm.nih.gov/17063641/.

Mandal, Shyamapada, and Manisha DebMandal. "Thyme (Thymus Vulgaris L.) Oils." *Essential Oils in Food Preservation, Flavor and Safety*, Academic Press, 30 Oct. 2015, www.sciencedirect.com/science/article/pii/B9780124166417000948.

Salehi B;Mishra AP;Shukla I;Sharifi-Rad M;Contreras MDM;Segura-Carretero A;Fathi H;Nasrabadi NN;Kobarfard F;Sharifi-Rad J; "Thymol, Thyme, and Other Plant Sources: Health and Potential Uses." *Phytotherapy Research : PTR*, U.S. National Library of Medicine, 2018, pubmed.ncbi.nlm.nih.gov/29785774/.

Salehi, Bahare, et al. "Thymol, Thyme, and Other Plant Sources: Health and Potential Uses." *Wiley Online Library*, John Wiley & Sons, Ltd, 22 May 2018, onlinelibrary.wiley.com/doi/abs/10.1002/ptr.6109.

Segvić Klarić M;Kosalec I;Mastelić J;Piecková E;Pepeljnak S; "Antifungal Activity of Thyme (Thymus Vulgaris L.) Essential Oil and Thymol against Moulds from Damp Dwellings." *Letters in Applied Microbiology*, U.S. National Library of Medicine, 2007, pubmed.ncbi.nlm.nih.gov/17209812/.

"Thyme May Be Better for Acne than Prescription Creams." *ScienceDaily*, ScienceDaily, 27 Mar. 2012, www.sciencedaily.com/releases/2012/03/120327215951.htm.

Valerian

Benke D;Barberis A;Kopp S;Altmann KH;Schubiger M;Vogt KE;Rudolph U;Möhler H; "GABA A Receptors as in Vivo Substrate for the Anxiolytic Action of Valerenic Acid, a Major Constituent of Valerian Root Extracts." *Neuropharmacology*, U.S. National Library of Medicine, 2009, pubmed.ncbi.nlm.nih.gov/18602406/.

PJ;, Houghton. "The Scientific Basis for the Reputed Activity of Valerian." *The Journal of Pharmacy and Pharmacology*, U.S. National Library of Medicine, 1999, pubmed.ncbi.nlm. nih.gov/10411208/.

RH;, Murphy K;Kubin ZJ;Shepherd JN;Ettinger. "Valeriana Officinalis Root Extracts Have Potent Anxiolytic Effects in Laboratory Rats." *Phytomedicine : International Journal of Phytotherapy and Phytopharmacology*, U.S. National Library of Medicine, 2010, pubmed. ncbi.nlm.nih.gov/20042323/.

Yarrow
....

de Sousa, Damião Pergentino, et al. "A Systematic Review of the Anxiolytic-Like Effects of Essential Oils in Animal Models." *Molecules (Basel, Switzerland)*, MDPI, 14 Oct. 2015, www.ncbi.nlm.nih.gov/pmc/articles/PMC6332383/.

I;, Pirbalouti AG;Koohpayeh A;Karimi. "The Wound Healing Activity of Flower Extracts of Punica Granatum and Achillea Kellalensis in Wistar Rats." *Acta Poloniae Pharmaceutica*, U.S. National Library of Medicine, 2010, pubmed.ncbi.nlm.nih.gov/20210088/.

Tadić V;Arsić I;Zvezdanović J;Zugić A;Cvetković D;Pavkov S; "The Estimation of the Traditionally Used Yarrow (Achillea Millefolium L. Asteraceae) Oil Extracts with Anti-Inflamatory Potential in Topical Application." *Journal of Ethnopharmacology*, U.S. National Library of Medicine, 2017, pubmed.ncbi.nlm.nih.gov/28163113/.